BRUNCH
GALORE

BRUNCH
GALORE

SARA LEWIS

spruce

An Hachette UK Company
First published in Great Britain in 2010 by Spruce
a division of Octopus Publishing Group Ltd
Endeavour House, 189 Shaftesbury Avenue,
London, WC2H 8JY
www.octopusbooks.co.uk
www.octopusbooksusa.com

Distributed in the U.S.A. and Canada for Octopus
Books USA
c/- Hachette Book Group USA
237 Park Avenue
New York, NY 10017

Copyright © Octopus Publishing Group Ltd 2010

Photography: Ian Garlick
Food Styling: Sara Lewis
Page Layout: Leigh Jones

ISBN 13 978-1-84601-371-3
ISBN 10 1-84601-371-2

A CIP catalog record for this book is available
from the British Library.

Printed and bound in China

10 9 8 7 6 5 4 3 2 1

Notes from the publisher

This book includes dishes made with nuts and nut
derivatives. It is advisable for those with known
allergic reactions to nuts and nut derivatives and
those who may be potentially vulnerable to these
allergies, such as pregnant and nursing mothers,
invalids, the elderly, babies, and children, to avoid
dishes make with nuts and nut oils. It is also
prudent to check the labels of already-prepared
ingredients for the possible inclusion of nut
derivatives.

Ovens should be preheated to the specific
temperature. If using a fan-assisted oven, follow
the manufacturer's instructions for adjusting the
time and temperature.

All waffle recipes have been made in a four
rectangular section waffle machine.

Fresh herbs have been used unless otherwise
stated.

Medium eggs have been used throughout.

This book contains some dishes made with raw or
lightly cooked eggs. It is prudent for more
vulnerable people, such as pregnant and nursing
mothers, invalids, the elderly, babies, and young
children, to avoid raw or lightly cooked eggs.

CONTENTS

INTRODUCTION

Nutritionists always stress the importance of eating a good breakfast first thing in the morning, but there never seems to be quite enough time to enjoy this first meal of the day and it can all too easily become nothing more than a refueling stop.

Thankfully weekends and vacations are different—breakfast can be enjoyed much later in the day and in a much slower and more relaxed way, so that it almost rolls on into lunch, becoming quite literally one meal —hence the name.

★ ORIGINS ★

The true origins of "brunch" are a little hazy, with Americans stating that it all started after the *New York Morning Sun* newspaper reporters christened their late breakfast "brunch," around 1906–1919, while in Britain it is thought that the word was coined in 1896 in the publication *Hunter's Weekly*.

★ A RELAXED STYLE OF ENTERTAINING ★

Regardless of its origins, brunch has become popular in America, where special Sunday brunch menus are commonplace in restaurants, and now it is growing in popularity in the UK, too. Unlike dinner, brunch is a more informal meal and can be a great way to get together with family and friends, over a buffet-style meal around the kitchen table or eaten alfresco in summer.

Because the food is so varied, there is something for everyone, whatever their age, from waffles and pancakes to baked sausages, bacon, and eggs or fruit biscuits and breads served warm from the oven. Who

Do your food shopping and as much food preparation as you can and store in the refrigerator the day before. Even if you don't lay the table the night before, put as much as you can ready on a tray, then it is one less thing to do in the morning. For larger gatherings it can be fun if friends bring a dish so that the workload and cost is shared.

can resist homemade baked beans on toast, pigs in blankets, or hot pancakes topped with Chantilly cream, bananas, and a drizzle of chocolate sauce?

As a more casual occasion, sitting down to brunch suits a gathering with young children, giving friends the chance to get together without the need for babysitters, and the choice of dishes can be tailored easily to suit all budgets.

★ GETTING AHEAD ★

By the very nature of brunch, it is a meal served late morning, so it's best to try and make some recipes the night before and then just do the minimum amount of cooking the next day leaving you to be just as relaxed as your diners.

★ ADDED EXTRAS ★

Don't feel that you must make everything on the table yourself—brunch is a relaxed, informal meal. If making the main course, then opt to buy croissants and jelly, or bagels, cream cheese, and smoked salmon. If you are having an appetizer, then arrange fruit attractively in a large bowl instead of making a fruit course or dessert, and let your diners help themselves. For a crowd, offer a selection of ham on a large platter together with a small bowl of pickles or chutneys or a selection of cheeses with some grapes, apples, or figs alongside your homemade items.

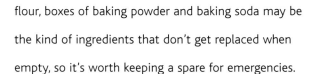

Buy, heat, and serve bread rolls and cook on the morning for that wonderful smell of baking if you would rather not make biscuits or cakes.

★ STOCKING YOUR PANTRY ★

While it can be enjoyable to plan for a brunch to share with friends it can also be good to rustle up an impromptu meal for just the family. This needn't mean a trip to the store.

EGGS

If you have a carton of eggs, you can quickly prepare a meal, from oven-baked egg and fries flavored with paprika, turmeric, and fennel to Spanish baked eggs or a summery frittata with asparagus.

PANCAKES & WAFFLES

Pancakes and waffles can be made with the most basic of ingredients—just a couple of eggs, some flour, and milk. Cartons of ultrapasteurized milk make a handy addition to any pantry and, while you are sure to have

flour, boxes of baking powder and baking soda may be the kind of ingredients that don't get replaced when empty, so it's worth keeping a spare for emergencies.

Both pancakes and waffles can be drizzled with a little honey or maple syrup and sprinkled with nuts, diced chocolate, or dried fruit. Frozen fruit, such as raspberries, cherries, or blueberries, also make great standbys and can be either defrosted in the microwave or warmed in a saucepan with a little water. Serve with spoonfuls of whipped cream, yogurt, or ice cream.

For savory fillings try shredded or sliced cheese, ham, or crispy bacon and a spoonful of cranberry sauce or chutney. From the freezer, salmon, shrimp, or mixed shellfish can be stirred into a light cheese sauce or, for a cheat's sauce, warm some cream cheese mixed with a little milk and fresh chopped herbs from the garden. Defrost frozen fish at room temperature by soaking in cold (never warm) water or in the microwave. Rinse with cold water and drain before use.

BAKES

Running low on bread? Then make up a batch of biscuits—the wonderful smell of baking will quickly draw the family into the kitchen.

COOKING FOR A CROWD

The majority of the recipes in the book are for four servings—with the exception of the cakes and bakes. If you plan to have more guests, simply multiply up the recipes to suit. The pancake recipes tend to make eight small pancakes—if feeding a crowd, the chances are your guests would just take one each, so one recipe quantity would serve eight if other recipes were served for this course. Again, when making biscuits or crepes, you may also find that your guests take just one or two.

★ MAKE A PLAN ★

First choose the recipes that you want to serve, then calculate how many pieces each one makes. Imagine these pieces on appetizer, main course, and dessert plates to help you gauge the total amount of food. Often the more choice you have, the smaller the portions that your guests will take, because they will try a little of everything. To help you with your planning, here are a few menus ideas.

SUMMER BRUNCH PARTY

Green eggs and ham cups

Salmon kedgeree

Fruit salad kebabs

WINTER BIRTHDAY BRUNCH

Parsley potato hot cakes with bacon

Spanish eggs

Chocolate and orange torte

MOTHER'S DAY BRUNCH

Melon with gingered green tea

Pigs in blankets

Chocolate peppermint waffles

VEGETARIAN BRUNCH

Quinoa and golden raisin porridge

Summer vegetable frittata

Chocolate cherry crepes

Carrot and honey bread

MAKE-AHEAD BRUNCH

Seafood pancake pie

Oven-baked pecan French toast

Prunes in tea with orange yogurt

Marzipan tea loaf

HOW TO MAKE WAFFLES

Made with a mix of flour, melted butter, eggs, and milk, waffles can be quickly whipped together in just a matter of minutes.

They can then be topped with a range of sweet or savory ingredients, ranging from Brie and cranberry sauce or ham and melted cheese to maple syrup, walnuts, and honeyed figs or baked clementines.

The secret of a really good waffle is use all-purpose flour with a mix of baking powder and baking soda to ensure a light, fluffy waffle. Beat with an egg, milk, buttermilk, coconut milk, even beer, to make a thick batter similar to that for drop biscuits or pancakes.

Sweeten, if desired, and enrich with a little butter or oil, depending on the recipe. Try to cook the batter as

soon after making as possible to maximize the effects of the added raising agent. Serve the waffles straight from the waffle machine with the flavoring of your choice and be as creative as you or the contents of your refrigerator will permit.

★ BUYING A WAFFLE MACHINE ★

Waffle irons were traditionally made as two hinged iron plates that were heated on the stove top and then filled with a thick batter. These are still available but have been superseded by electric waffle machines. Quicker and easier to use, they come with a thermostatically controlled, variable heat setting, lights to tell you when the machine is hot enough, and an audible beep to let you know when the waffles are cooked. As with any electrical kitchen gadget, waffle machines come in a

range of prices and sizes and can make anything from two to four, even six, waffles at a time.

The most widely available machines tend to make four rectangular waffles, but some models can make fan-shape and even heart-shape waffles. Unlike a manual waffle iron, most models do not require you to turn the waffles during cooking because there are heating elements on the top and bottom of the machine.

MAKING THE RIGHT CHOICE

To help you decide on which model to buy, try to imagine how often you will use it. If it is just for the occasional brunch party, then choose one of the lower-priced makes. Some models have detachable nonstick plates that not only make cleaning easier but can be interchanged with a sandwich toasting plate. They do tend to be a little more expensive but it does mean that you have two machines in one, so it is more versatile.

★ USING THE MACHINE FOR THE FIRST TIME ★

Always read your manufacturer's handbook, because some recommend that the waffle plates are primed before use—which just means that they must be greased and then heated without any waffle batter added the first time that you use the machine. Some manufacturers may also recommend greasing the plates each time you make waffles. The easiest way to grease the plates is to use a spray vegetable or olive oil. Alternately, you can use a pastry brush dipped in oil.

Make sure to preheat your waffle machine and to adjust the heat setting (see the manufacturer's handbook for correct setting). Depending on the model, this can take between 5 and 10 minutes, so prepare the waffle batter while the machine heats up.

★ COOKING THE WAFFLES ★

Once the light has gone out or the beeper has sounded, scoop the batter into the center of the waffle plate —don't be tempted to overfill, or the batter will spill out during cooking. The weight of the machine lid will spread out the batter. The recipes in the book will make four rectangular waffles, so adjust the amount of batter depending on the size of your own machine—or cook in two or more batches if needed.

As a general guide, the waffles will be done when the steaming stops. However, if you are not sure, lift the lid a little—they should be well risen and golden brown. If the waffles stick to the plates you will usually find that they are not quite ready.

Ease the waffles out of the machine using a nonstick spatula so that you don't scratch the plates. Transfer to serving plates and serve with your chosen topping.

Cook additional waffles as needed and remember to turn the machine off when finished.

★ CLEANING ★

To clean the plates, if detachable, remove them, then wash in warm soapy water with a soft cloth, rinse, and dry. If they are not removeables, wipe with a clean damp cloth and rub away any batter spills from the side of the machine with a cloth or scrape away stubborn marks with a nonstick spatula. Never immerse the machine in hot water.

HOW TO MAKE PANCAKES

Pancakes fall into two categories: thin lacy pancakes, most often called crepes, and the thicker pancakes known to Americans, also called hotcakes, griddle cakes, or drop biscuits.

★ MAKING GOOD CREPES ★

A good skillet is just as important as the batter when it comes to making a good crepe. Seasoning and cleaning it properly are also important.

CHOOSING A PAN

Invest in a good skillet—a traditional crepe pan has very low sides but a standard-shaped skillet with sloping sides will work just as well. Most sweet crepes are made in a 7-inch skillet, while savory ones tend to be larger. Choose a heavy nonstick skillet with a handle that stays cool. Cast-iron skillets are also available but make sure to season the skillet the first time that you use it by heating and rubbing with salt. Wipe the skillet clean with paper towels, then heat it with a little oil and wipe clean once again. Wipe the skillet rather than wash it after use to keep it in a good condition.

MAKING THE BATTER

• Sift the all-purpose flour into a bowl for lightness. Make a well in the center and add the whole egg and egg yolk. Add a tablespoon of oil or melted butter if you want to enrich the batter. You can also flavor the batter with a little salt, sugar, vanilla extract, grated fruit zest, ground spices, or cocoa powder.

• Gradually beat in the milk, little by little, until it forms a smooth batter. A mixture of milk and water can be used instead, but it will make the pancakes more difficult to handle when cooking. Or try buttermilk if you prefer a richer flavor.

- Let the batter rest for 15 minutes so that the flour can soften and swell. Resting will also produce a more elastic batter that will coat the bottom of the pan effectively and reduce the possibility of the batter tearing. The longer the batter stands, the thicker it will get. Thin pancakes, or crepes, should have a batter that is the consistency of light cream, so, if your batter has been standing for longer than 30 minutes, it may need thinning with a little extra milk or water.

COOKING THE CREPES

- Heat a little sunflower oil or vegetable oil in the pan; pour off the excess into a small bowl.
- Add 2–3 tablespoons of the batter to the center of the skillet. Tilt the skillet until the batter coats the

TIP

Crepes can be cooked the night before and stacked, interleaved with squares of nonstick parchment paper or wax paper to stop them from sticking together. Wrap in foil and keep in the refrigerator. Reheat as a stack of no more than eight pancakes, wrapped in greased foil in a low oven, or by cooking individually for a minute or two in a hot skillet. If you intend to reheat crepes in a skillet, cook them until only lightly browned the first time around, so that they will not be overcooked when reheated.

bottom thinly. Less really is more in this instance—imagine you are making a thin lacy material. Fill in any gaps with a little extra batter if you need to and cook for 1–2 minutes, until the underside is golden brown.

- Loosen the edge of the crepe with a spatula, then turn over, or flip if you prefer. Cook the second side

preheat the skillet or griddle before use—to test the heat, drop a little water onto the ungreased skillet. If the water forms little jumping balls, it is ready; if it settles and foams, it is too cool; and if the droplets immediately evaporate, it is too hot.

COOKING DROP BISCUITS

As with crepes, you need only a tiny amount of oil when frying. If using a skillet, add about one tablespoon of oil, heat, and then pour off the excess into a small bowl. For a griddle, moisten a piece of folded paper towel with oil and then carefully rub it over the hot flat griddle plate.

These pancakes are thicker, and so it is important not to have the skillet too hot or they will be ready on the outside before the center is cooked through. To test if the cakes are ready, break one in half to double check that it is cooked right through.

Remove the pancake from the skillet and keep it hot in a folded napkin or dish towel while cooking the remaining mixture.

until golden then slide the crepe out of the skillet and repeat until all the batter is used.

• Repeat the process, oiling the skillet as needed and making crepes until all the batter is used up.

★ DROP BISCUITS & PANCAKES ★

Made with ingredients similar to those used in crepes, this batter has less milk, so it has a consistency similar to waffle batter. It contains an added raising agent in the form of self-rising flour, baking powder, or baking soda and must be cooked the minute that the batter is made.

Traditionally, these cakes are cooked on a griddle or girdle, a heavy, flat cast-iron disk with a curved handle, but they can also be made in a large skillet. Always

BIG BRUNCH
SPECIALS

RED FLANNEL HASH

Rather than being fried on the stove top, these potatoes are baked in the oven with chunky pieces of beet and red onion—hence the name—then topped with a fried egg. Serve with ketchup or tomato relish for an easy brunch come lunch.

SERVES 4

6 medium potatoes, about 1½ lb
5 tablespoons sunflower oil
1 large red onion, roughly chopped
1¾ cooked, peeled beets, cut into
   large chunks
2 bay leaves
4 eggs
1 teaspoon mustard powder
1 teaspoon paprika, plus a little extra
   to garnish
Salt and cayenne pepper

1. Preheat the oven to 400°F.

2. Bring a large saucepan of water to a boil. Peel and cut the potatoes into 1-inch cubes, then add to the water and boil for 3–4 minutes, until just tender.

3. Pour 4 tablespoons of the oil into a roasting pan and warm in the preheated oven for 3–4 minutes.

4. Drain the potatoes and rough up the edges by shaking in the colander. Add to the hot oil with the onion, beet, and bay leaves. Season with salt and cayenne pepper, sprinkle with the mustard and paprika, then toss in the oil.

5. Bake in the preheated oven for 35–40 minutes, stirring the vegetables once or twice so that they brown evenly. When they are almost ready, heat the remaining oil in a skillet, add the eggs, and fry until the whites are set and the yolks are still runny.

6. Spoon the hash onto plates, top with the eggs, and sprinkle with a little extra paprika, if liked. Serve immediately.

SUMMER VEGETABLE FRITTATA

SERVES 4–6

Butter for greasing
1 cup asparagus tips
4 oz sugar snap peas
¾ cup shelled fava beans, defrosted
   if frozen
1 medium zucchini, sliced
4 scallions, chopped
Small bunch of fresh basil, larger
   leaves torn into pieces
8 eggs
¼ cup freshly grated Parmesan
   cheese
1 cup sour cream
Salt and ground black pepper

RED PEPPER SAUCE

5 oz roasted red bell peppers from
   a jar, drained
1 tomato, roughly chopped
3 tablespoons slivered almonds
1 thin slice stale bread without crusts
1 small garlic clove
3 tablespoons olive oil
2 teaspoons red wine vinegar
1 teaspoon tomato paste
Pinch of smoked paprika or
   chilli powder

1. Preheat the oven to 350°F. Butter a 6-cup, 2-inch deep ovenproof dish.

2. Bring a saucepan of water to a boil. Add the asparagus, sugar snap peas, fava beans, and zucchini. Cover and cook for 2 minutes then drain well.

3. Turn the vegetables into the buttered ovenproof dish and add the scallions and basil.

4. Beat the eggs, Parmesan, and sour cream together in a bowl with a fork. Season with salt and black pepper, then pour over the vegetables and gently mix together. Sprinkle with a little extra ground black pepper, then bake in the preheated oven for 25–30 minutes, until the top is golden and the frittata is set.

5. Meanwhile, put all the sauce ingredients into a blender or food processor and blend until smooth. Transfer to a small serving bowl.

6. Allow the frittata to stand for 5 minutes, then cut into pieces and transfer to serving plates. Serve with spoonfuls of sauce and warm crusty bread.

BRUNCH PIZZA

SERVES 4

1 cup warm water

1 teaspoon superfine sugar

2 teaspoons active dry yeast
(not instant dry yeast)

3 cups bread flour

1 teaspoon salt

2 tablespoons olive oil

TOMATO SAUCE

1 onion, finely chopped

1 tablespoon olive oil

1¾ cups canned chopped tomatoes

1 teaspoon superfine sugar

1–2 garlic cloves, finely chopped
(optional)

Small bunch of basil

Salt and ground black pepper

TOPPING

2⅔ cups sliced mushrooms

6 vacuum-packed frankfurters,
thickly sliced

4 slices of Canadian-style bacon,
each cut into 3 pieces

2 balls mozzarella cheese, 4 oz each,
drained and torn into pieces

1. Pour ¾ cup warm water into a bowl, sprinkle the sugar and yeast over the top, and stir. Let stand in a warm place for 10–15 minutes, until the yeast has formed a thick frothy layer on top of the water.

2. Put the flour and salt in a mixing bowl, add the oil, then stir in the yeast mixture to form a soft but not sticky dough, adding the remaining warm water if needed.

3. Turn onto a work surface and knead well for 5 minutes, then lightly flour the bowl and put the dough back into it. Cover with oiled plastic wrap and transfer to the refrigerator to rise overnight.

4. Make the tomato sauce by frying the onion in the oil for 5 minutes until softened. Add the tomatoes, sugar, garlic, if using, and a few torn basil leaves. Season with a little salt and black pepper, then simmer for 10–15 minutes, until thick. Let cool and store in the refrigerator.

5. Next morning, knead the risen bread dough once again. Cut into four pieces and roll each piece out thinly into a rough circle about 8 inches in diameter. Divide the dough circles between two large oiled baking sheets, cover loosely with oiled plastic wrap, and let stand in a warm place for 40–50 minutes until risen.

6. Preheat the oven to 425°F. Remove the plastic wrap, spoon tomato sauce over the bases, then divide the remaining topping ingredients between the pizzas, reserving the basil for garnish.

7. Bake the pizzas in the preheated oven for about 10 minutes, until golden. Sprinkle with the remaining basil leaves.

EGG WHITE OMELET WITH SMOKED SALMON

A Sunday brunch doesn't have to mean piling on the calories, as this low-fat egg white omelet, generously topped with cottage cheese and folds of smoked salmon, proves.

SERVES 4

TOPPING
1½ cups cottage cheese
2 tomatoes, diced
Bunch of scallions, finely chopped
Grated zest of 1 lemon
¼ cup chopped fresh dill, plus extra
   sprigs to garnish
7 oz sliced smoked salmon

OMELET
12 egg whites
2 tablespoons chopped fresh
   dill weed
Olive oil spray
Salt and ground black pepper

1. Preheat the broiler. Spoon the cottage cheese into a serving bowl. Mix the tomatoes, scallions, and lemon zest in a second bowl and arrange the smoked salmon on a plate.

2. To make the omelet, beat half the egg whites until they form moist-looking peaks, then fold in one-quarter of the dill and season with a little salt and black pepper.

3. Spray a 7-inch omelet pan with a little oil and heat. Add half the beaten egg whites to the pan and cook over medium heat until the underside is golden. Transfer to the broiler and cook until the top is golden and the egg whites set.

4. Loosen the omelet with a spatula, then slide out onto a serving plate. Top with one-quarter of the cottage cheese, tomato mix, and smoked salmon and serve immediately garnished with a few sprigs of dill. Quickly repeat to make a second omelet with the remaining beaten egg whites, then make two more in the same way, serving each one as it is ready.

BIG MAC 'N' CHEESE

Macaroni and cheese is one of those comforting dishes that always remind you of home, served here with a surprise layer of just-wilted spinach.

SERVES 6

8 oz macaroni
3½ cups baby leaf spinach
Pinch of grated nutmeg
4 tablespoons butter
¼ cup all-purpose flour
2½ cups milk
2 teaspoons Dijon mustard
1¾ cups shredded cheddar cheese
4 small tomatoes, about 14 oz, cut
   into wedges
2 tablespoons fresh bread crumbs
Salt and ground black pepper

1. Preheat the broiler. Bring a large saucepan of water to a boil and add the macaroni. Bring back to a boil and simmer for 10–12 minutes, until tender, or according to package directions.

2. Rinse the spinach with water, roughly drain, then add to a hot skillet and cook for 2 minutes, until just wilted. Press out any water, then spoon the spinach into the bottom of a shallow ovenproof dish. Season with a little salt, black pepper, and nutmeg.

3. Drain the pasta into a colander. Dry the saucepan, then add the butter and heat until melted. Stir in the flour, then gradually add the milk and bring to a boil, stirring constantly, until thickened.

4. Stir in the mustard, three-quarters of the cheese, and plenty of salt and black pepper and heat until the cheese has melted. Stir in the macaroni and reheat if necessary, then mix in three-quarters of the tomatoes.

5. Spoon the macaroni mixture over the spinach, arrange the remaining tomatoes over the top, then sprinkle with the remaining cheese and the bread crumbs. Cook under the broiler until golden, then spoon onto plates and serve with broiled bacon, if liked.

CAJUN MEATLOAF

This American favorite is mixed with allspice, ginger, paprika, and chile for a meatloaf with a kick. Serve with salad or, if you feel extra hungry, try with the homemade baked beans on page 134. Any leftovers are good cold in a lunchbox.

SERVES 4–6

8 oz bacon

1 lb lean ground beef

4 large pork sausages, skins removed

2¼ cups fresh bread crumbs

1 teaspoon ground allspice

1 teaspoon ground ginger

1 teaspoon paprika

¼ teaspoon crushed hot red pepper
or dried chile flakes

2 teaspoons tomato paste

2 teaspoons fresh thyme leaves

1 onion, finely chopped

½ red bell pepper, cored, seeded,
and diced

½ green bell pepper, cored, seeded,
and diced

1 egg

Salt and ground black pepper

1. Preheated oven at 350°F. Lightly oil a 9 x 5 x 3-inch loaf pan and line the bottom and two long sides with a piece of nonstick parchment paper.

2. Stretch each slice of bacon until half as long again, then use about three-quarters to line the bottom and sides of the pan, reserving enough to cover the top later.

3. Put the beef and sausage meat into a mixing bowl and add the bread crumbs, spices, tomato paste, and thyme. Add the vegetables, the egg, and a generous sprinkling of salt and black pepper, then mix together well.

4. Spoon the beef mixture into the bacon-lined pan and press down firmly. Fold the edges of the bacon over the top, then cover with the reserved bacon. Cover the top of the pan with foil, then stand it in a roasting pan. Pour enough hot water into the roasting pan to come halfway up the sides of the loaf pan then cook in the preheated oven for 1 hour or until the meatloaf is cooked through.

5. Take the loaf pan out of the water and let stand for 15 minutes to firm up. Loosen the edges with a round-bladed knife, then turn out onto a plate with a rim and remove the lining paper. Cut into thick slices and serve warm with salad. If serving cold, leave in the loaf pan to chill before turning out.

SPICED EGG & ROAST ROOT VEGETABLES

We all love egg and French fries but this turmeric, fennel, and paprika spiced version made with baking potatoes, sweet potatoes, and parsnips is oven baked, so not only is it lower in fat but it avoids the smell of deep-frying in the kitchen.

SERVES 4

6 medium baking potatoes,
   about 1½ lb
3 medium sweet potatoes, about 1 lb
3 medium parsnips, about 12 oz
¼ cup olive oil
1 teaspoon paprika
1 teaspoon turmeric
1 teaspoon fennel seeds
Coarse sea salt and cayenne pepper
4 eggs

1. Preheat the oven to 400°F. Peel and cut all the vegetables into chunky fries. Bring a saucepan of water to a boil and add the pieces of baking potato. Parboil for 3–4 minutes, until almost tender.

2. Meanwhile, pour the oil into a large roasting pan and heat in the oven for 3–4 minutes.

3. Drain the potatoes and rough up the edges by shaking in the colander. Turn into the pan of hot oil and add the sweet potatoes and parsnips. Sprinkle with the spices, fennel seeds, and a little coarse sea salt and cayenne pepper and toss in the oil.

4. Roast in the preheated oven at 400°F for 30–35 minutes, stirring once or twice, until browned around the edges.

5. Make a large indentation in the center of the pan, break the eggs into the space, then return the pan to the oven for 5 minutes, until the eggs are just cooked. Transfer to serving plates and drizzle any juices from the bottom of the pan over the eggs. Serve immediately with a little ketchup.

MINI BACON & EGG CUPS

These egg cups are very easy and quick to prepare and are full of flavor. As a breakfast or brunch item, these are just as good served hot from the oven as wrapped in foil and taken on a picnic brunch in a bicycle basket, or seaside picnic in a backpack.

SERVES 4–6

Butter for greasing
12 slices of bacon
4 plum tomatoes, sliced
   (24 slices needed)
2 tablespoons tomato chutney
6 eggs
¾ cup sour cream
2 tablespoons chopped chives
   (optional)
Salt and ground black pepper

1. Preheat the oven to 350°F. Lightly butter a 12-cup nonstick muffin pan and line the sides of each cup with a slice of bacon. Add a slice of tomato to the bottom and dot the chutney on top.

2. With a fork, beat the eggs, sour cream, and chives together in a bowl. Season with salt and black pepper and divide evenly between the cups of the muffin pan.

3. Top with the remaining tomato slices and cook in the preheated oven for 20 minutes, until well risen, golden, and set.

4. Let stand for 5 minutes, then loosen the edges with a round-bladed knife and remove from the pan. Serve warm or cold.

PANZANELLA

Originating from Tuscany, Italy, this is a popular summer dish, with the toasted bread soaking up the juices from the tomato and olive oil and vinegar dressing. The riper the tomatoes, the more juice there will be, and the more delicious the dish.

SERVES 4

4 slices of ciabatta bread,
   lightly toasted
4 ripe tomatoes
½ cucumber, seeded and peeled
1 red onion
Handful of chopped flat-leaf parsley
1 tablespoon chopped black olives
¼ cup extra virgin olive oil
1–2 tablespoons wine vinegar
Juice of ½ lemon
Salt and ground black pepper

1. Cut or tear the bread into small pieces and place them in a large bowl.

2. Remove the green core from the tomatoes. Cut up the tomatoes and add to the pieces of bread.

3. Cut the cucumber into quarters lengthwise and then into cubes. Add to the bowl with the tomatoes and bread. Chop the onion and add to the salad with the parsley and olives.

4. Mix together the oil, vinegar, and lemon juice and season with salt and black pepper. Pour the dressing over the salad and mix well. Cover and let stand at room temperature for at least 1 hour before serving, to let all the flavors mingle.

SALMON KEDGEREE

An Indian-inspired breakfast, kedgeree was made popular in England by those returning from postings abroad. Traditionally made with smoked haddock, this version made with salmon gently poached in a coconut broth tastes even better.

SERVES 4

2 tablespoons butter
1 onion, chopped
1 teaspoon turmeric
5 cardamom pods, crushed
2 small bay leaves
1 generous cup instant brown rice
1¾ cups coconut milk
3 large salmon fillets, about 1 lb
3 eggs
Small bunch of cilantro, roughly
    chopped
Salt and ground black pepper

1. Heat the butter in a deep skillet, add the onion, and fry gently for 5 minutes, stirring, until softened but not browned.

2. Stir in the turmeric, cardamom pods and their black seeds, and the bay leaves. Cook for 1 minute, then stir in the rice and add the coconut milk and 1 cup water. Season with salt and black pepper and mix well.

3. Lay the fish in the skillet in a single layer, then bring to a boil, partially cover the skillet with a lid, and simmer for 10 minutes, until the fish is cooked and flakes when pressed with a knife.

4. Lift the salmon out of the skillet with a spatula, transfer to a plate, then peel away the skin, break into flakes, and discard any bones. Continue cooking the rice for an additional 15–20 minutes, uncovered and stirring occasionally, until the rice is tender and nearly all the liquid has been absorbed.

5. Meanwhile, put the eggs into a small saucepan, cover with cold water, and bring to a boil. Simmer for 8 minutes. Drain, rinse with cold water until cool enough to handle, then crack and shell the eggs and quarter.

6. Return the salmon to the skillet. Add the eggs and gently reheat. Sprinkle with the cilantro and spoon into shallow bowls. Serve immediately.

QUESADILLAS

Similar to a giant toasted sandwich, these quesadillas are made with soft flour tortillas and filled with a chunky cheese, tomato, onion, and avocado mix flavored with a little chile and cilantro. Vary the filling to suit your family and try with sliced mushrooms, ham, even spinach.

SERVES 4

1 small red onion, finely chopped

1 green bell pepper, cored, seeded, and diced

2 tomatoes, diced

½ cup corn kernels, drained if canned, defrosted if frozen

1 mild red chile, seeded and finely chopped

2 ripe avocados, halved, pitted, and peeled

Juice of 1 lime

Small bunch of cilantro

1⅓ cups coarsely shredded cheddar cheese

8 large, soft flour tortillas

Sunflower oil for frying

Sour cream, to serve

1. Place the onion, green pepper, tomatoes, corn, and chile in a bowl and stir together.

2. Dice the avocados and toss with the lime juice. Roughly chop half the cilantro. Add both to the vegetables with the shredded cheese and gently mix together.

3. Lay four tortillas out on the work surface and divide the vegetable mixture between them. Cover with the remaining tortillas and press together lightly.

4. Heat a little oil in a skillet with a bottom a little larger than the tortilla. Pour off the excess oil, then carefully lift one quesadilla into the skillet and cook over medium heat, pressing the top tortilla down and the edges together with the back of a spatula until the underside is blistered golden brown. Turn over, being careful that the filling does not fall out, and repeat with the second side.

5. Transfer to a cutting board and cook the remaining quesadillas in the same way.

6. Cut into triangles and serve with spoonfuls of sour cream and sprigs of the remaining cilantro.

CHUNKY SALMON & CRAB CAKES

SERVES 4

FISH CAKES
5 medium potatoes, about 1¼ lb
2 salmon fillets, about 13 oz
2 tablespoons butter
2–3 tablespoons milk
Grated zest and juice of ½ lemon
4 scallions, finely chopped
6 oz canned white crabmeat, drained
Flour for dusting
2 eggs
2¾ cups fresh bread crumbs
Salt and ground black pepper

TARTAR SAUCE
¼ cup mayonnaise
¼ cup low-fat plain yogurt
Grated zest of ½ lemon
1 tablespoon drained capers, chopped
1 tablespoon chopped fresh tarragon

TO FINISH
2 tablespoons butter
2–3 tablespoons sunflower oil
1 lemon, cut into wedges
Green salad, to serve

1. Pour water into the bottom of a saucepan into which a steaming basket fits and bring to a boil. Peel the potatoes, cut into chunks, and add to the water. Insert the steaming basket, place the salmon on this, then cover and cook the salmon for 8–10 minutes and the potatoes for 10–15 minutes, depending on the size of the chunks.

2. Remove the skin from the salmon, break it into chunks, and discard any bones. Drain the potatoes, mash with the butter and milk, then add the lemon zest, lemon juice, and scallions. Season with salt and pepper.

3. Fold the salmon chunks and crab into the potato, then spoon the mixture into eight mounds on a cutting board. With floured hands, shape into eight thick patties.

4. Beat the eggs with 2 tablespoons water and a little salt and pepper in a shallow dish. Put the bread crumbs into a second shallow dish. Dip each fish cake into the egg and then into the crumbs to coat all over. Chill until required.

5. To make the tartar sauce, mix all the ingredients with a little salt and pepper, then chill.

6. When ready to serve, divide the butter and oil between two skillets, or cook in batches, and fry the fish cakes for about 10 minutes until golden on both sides and hot through. Drain well and serve two per portion with a little dish of the tartar sauce, lemon wedges, and a green salad.

MACKEREL WITH LEMONS & OLIVES

Mackerel is bursting with plenty of healthy nutrients, so this dish is not only tasty, it is also great for you.

SERVES 4

4 mackerel, about 10 oz each, gutted
   and heads removed
Small bunch of thyme, bruised
1 teaspoon cumin seeds, bruised
2 tablespoons extra virgin olive oil,
   plus extra for drizzling
1 lemon, sliced
2 bay leaves
⅔ cup black olives
2 tablespoons lemon juice
Salt and ground black pepper
Tomato, basil, and onion salad,
   to serve

1. Preheat the oven to 425°F. Use a sharp knife to make three slashes in each side of each fish. Combine the thyme, cumin, and oil, season with salt and black pepper, and rub all over the fish, making sure some of the flavorings are pressed into the cuts.

2. Arrange the mackerel in a roasting pan and top with the lemon slices, bay leaves, and olives. Drizzle with the lemon juice and a little extra oil, season with salt and black pepper, and cook in the preheated oven for 15 minutes, until the fish are cooked through. Serve with a tomato, basil, and onion salad.

TIP
Bruising the thyme and cumin seeds will help to release their flavor. The easiest way to do this is by using a mortar and pestle, or on a cutting board with a rolling pin.

CAESAR SALAD

Serve this salad as an accompaniment to other savory brunch dishes, or if you want to simplify things, add some broiled chicken breast and eat it as a meal on its own.

SERVES 4

1 garlic clove, crushed
4 anchovy fillets, chopped
Juice of 1 lemon
2 teaspoons mustard powder
1 egg yolk
Ground black pepper
¾ cup extra virgin olive oil
Vegetable oil for frying
3 slices of country bread, cubed
1 romaine lettuce, torn into pieces
3 tablespoons freshly grated
   Parmesan cheese

1. Place the garlic, anchovy fillets, lemon juice, mustard, and egg yolk in a small mixing bowl and season with black pepper. With a handheld electric beater or small whisk, mix well until combined. Slowly drizzle in the olive oil, mixing all the time, to form a thick, creamy sauce. If the sauce becomes too thick, add a little water.

2. Heat the vegetable oil in a skillet. Test with a small piece of bread to see if it is hot enough; if it sizzles, add the bread cubes, turning them when they are golden. When they are cooked, transfer them to a plate lined with paper towels to absorb the excess oil.

3. Put the lettuce into a large bowl, pour over the dressing, sprinkle over 2 tablespoons of the Parmesan, and mix well.

4. Serve the salad in a large bowl or on individual plates, sprinkled with the croutons and the remaining Parmesan.

PIZZA BIANCHI

The Italians love Pizza Bianchi, piled high with pungent arugula leaves and a drizzle of extra virgin olive oil, rather than the usual cooked ingredients. This pizza is packed with fresh flavors and is perfect for summertime and eating outdoors.

SERVES 4

4 Mediterranean flatbreads, about
   8 inches each
7 oz Gorgonzola or dolcelatte cheese,
   crumbled
8 slices of prosciutto
1¼ cups wild arugula
Ground black pepper
Extra virgin olive oil for drizzling

1. Preheat the oven to 400°F. Place the flatbreads on two baking sheets and sprinkle the blue cheese over the centers.

2. Bake in the preheated oven for 6–7 minutes, until the cheese has melted and the bases are crisp.

3. Top the pizzas with the prosciutto and some arugula. Grind over some black pepper and drizzle with oil. Serve immediately.

COUNTRY SALAD

With the addition of hard-cooked eggs and fava beans, this country salad is both healthy and filling.

SERVES 4

2 eggs
1½ cups shelled fava beans, defrosted
   if frozen
1 cup halved green beans, about 4 oz
8 firm ripe plum tomatoes, cut
   into wedges
½ small cucumber, diced
2 celery ribs, sliced
1¼ cups diced cooked beets, about
   6 oz
1 small red onion, sliced thinly
2 tablespoons drained capers
DRESSING
2 tablespoons grated horseradish or
   1 tablespoon creamed horseradish
¼ cup extra virgin olive oil
2 teaspoons red wine vinegar
Pinch of sugar
2 tablespoons chopped parsley
Salt and ground black pepper

1. Put the eggs into a saucepan of water, bring to a boil, and cook for 8 minutes, until hard cooked. Cool in cold water, then crack and shell.

2. Blanch the fava beans and green beans in a saucepan of boiling salted water for 3 minutes then drain, refresh under cold water, and pat dry on paper towels.

3. Place the beans in a large bowl and add the tomatoes, cucumber, celery, beets, onion, and capers.

4. To make the dressing, mix together the horseradish, olive oil, vinegar, sugar, and parsley and season with salt and black pepper, to taste. Pour over the salad and toss gently until all the ingredients are evenly coated.

5. Transfer the salad to a serving dish and top with the eggs, cut lengthwise into quarters. Serve immediately.

GNOCCHI WITH CREAMY VEGETABLES

Completely meat-free, this brunch is quick and easy to put together. If serving to vegetarians, when buying the Parmesan check the label so that you can be assured that it does not contain rennet from an animal source.

SERVES 4

2 tablespoons butter
2 tablespoons olive oil
1 fennel bulb, diced, reserving the green feathery tops
1¾ cups diced butternut squash, about 8 oz
1 red onion, thinly sliced
1 tablespoon all-purpose flour
¼ cup dry white vermouth
2 cups vegetable stock
¼ cup heavy cream
1-lb package ready-made gnocchi
Salt and ground black pepper
Freshly shaved or grated Parmesan cheese, to serve

1. Heat the butter and oil in a large skillet, add the diced fennel, squash, and the onion and fry gently for 10 minutes, until softened.

2. Stir in the flour, then add the vermouth and stock. Bring to a boil, stirring, and simmer for 2–3 minutes until the vegetables are tender. Stir in the cream, season with salt and black pepper, and remove from the heat.

3. Bring a large saucepan of water to a boil, add the gnocchi, and cook for 3 minutes, until they have risen to the surface of the water and are piping hot. Drain and stir into the sauce.

4. Garnish the gnocchi with the reserved green, feathery fennel tops. Spoon into shallow dishes and serve with shaved or grated Parmesan.

CHEESY ROSTI

Crisp and golden potato cakes, topped with roasted mushrooms and poached eggs, make an indulgent vegetarian brunch. For a special occasion, add a dollop of sour cream and a sprinkling of chopped fresh chives.

SERVES 4

4 medium potatoes, about 1 lb, peeled and grated
1 onion, thinly sliced
1 tablespoon chopped fresh sage
1 cup shredded cheddar cheese
5 eggs
2 tablespoons extra virgin olive oil
4 large mushrooms
Salt and ground black pepper

1. Preheat the oven to 425°F. Place the grated potato in a fine-mesh strainer and squeeze out the excess liquid. Transfer to a large bowl, add the onion, sage, and cheese, and season with salt and black pepper.

2. Lightly beat one of the eggs, then add to the mixture and stir well until combined.

3. Heat half the oil in a large nonstick skillet, tip in the potato mixture, and cook over medium heat for about 12 minutes, until the underneath is browned.

4. Carefully slide the rosti out onto a large plate, upturn the skillet over the plate and use oven mitts to flip the skillet over, returning the rosti to the skillet. Cook for another 12 minutes, until browned on the second side.

5. Meanwhile, place the mushrooms, cap side down, in a roasting pan. Drizzle over the remaining oil, season with salt and black pepper, and roast in the preheated oven for 20 minutes, until the mushrooms are tender.

6. Just before serving, poach the remaining eggs in a pan of gently simmering water for 3 minutes, until cooked. Serve the rosti in wedges topped with a roasted mushroom and a poached egg.

HASHED SWEET POTATOES WITH EGGS

Sweet potatoes have a distinctive, earthy sweetness that goes well with bell peppers and onion. For this recipe, you could use half sweet potatoes and half ordinary potatoes, or even just ordinary potatoes if you prefer.

SERVES 2

2 medium sweet potatoes, about 12 oz

3 tablespoons olive or vegetable oil

1 red onion, chopped

1 garlic clove, crushed (optional)

2 teaspoons paprika

1 red bell pepper, cored, seeded, and chopped

1 green bell pepper, cored, seeded, and chopped

2 eggs

1. Preheat the broiler to a moderate heat. Scrub the sweet potatoes and cut them into ½-inch dice. Bring a saucepan of water to a boil, add the diced potatoes, and cook for 5 minutes, until softened. Drain thoroughly.

2. Heat the oil in a heavy skillet. Add the onion and sweet potatoes and fry gently for about 5 minutes, until beginning to brown. Add the garlic, if using, paprika, and bell pepper and fry for 5 minutes more.

3. When the vegetables are soft and pale golden, make two indentations in the mixture, each large enough to take an egg. Break an egg into each space and cook gently until set.

4. Place the skillet under the broiler to finish cooking the eggs, then serve immediately.

ROAST PUMPKIN WITH WALNUT PESTO

This flavorsome recipe is very quick to prepare. Choose a small, round pumpkin to make cutting easier. Any leftover pesto can be stored in an airtight container in the refrigerator for up to five days and tossed with spaghetti for a quick and simple supper dish.

SERVES 4

2 lb pumpkin or butternut squash
Extra virgin olive oil for brushing
Salt and ground black pepper
PESTO
1½ cups arugula leaves, plus extra
   to serve
½ cup walnuts, toasted
2 scallions, trimmed and chopped
1 large garlic clove, crushed
3 tablespoons walnut oil
3 tablespoons extra virgin olive oil

1. Preheat the oven to 425°F.

2. Leaving the skin on, cut the pumpkin into eight wedges and discard the seeds. Brush with oil, season with salt and black pepper, and place on a large baking sheet. Roast in the preheated oven for 20–25 minutes, until tender, turning the wedges halfway through.

3. Meanwhile, make the pesto. Combine the arugula, walnuts, scallions, and garlic in a food processor and blend until finely chopped. Gradually blend in the oils and season with salt and black pepper.

4. Serve the pumpkin with the pesto garnished with arugula leaves.

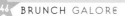
MEDITERRANEAN GOAT CHEESE OMELET

These omelets, filled with creamy goat cheese and served with warm, basil-scented tomatoes, have a real taste of the Mediterranean. It's a good idea to use a combination of red and yellow cherry tomatoes for maximum color impact.

SERVES 4

¼ cup extra virgin olive oil
3 cups cherry tomatoes, about 1 lb, halved
A little chopped fresh basil
12 eggs
2 tablespoons whole-grain mustard
4 tablespoons butter
4 oz soft goat cheese, diced
Salt and ground black pepper
Watercress, to garnish

1. Heat the oil in a skillet and fry the tomatoes for 2–3 minutes, until they have softened (if necessary, do this in two batches). Add the basil, season with salt and black pepper, transfer to a bowl, and keep warm.

2. Beat the eggs with the mustard and season with salt and black pepper. Melt a quarter of the butter in an omelet pan or small skillet, then swirl in a quarter of the egg mixture. Fork over the omelet so that it cooks evenly.

3. As soon as it is set on the bottom (but still a little runny in the middle), dot over a quarter of the goat cheese and cook for another 30 seconds. Carefully slide the omelet onto a warmed serving plate, folding it in half as you do so.

4. Repeat with the remaining mixture to make three more omelets. Serve with the tomatoes and garnish with watercress.

SPANISH EGGS

A colorful mix of Mediterranean vegetables flavored with rosemary and smoked paprika. If you haven't used smoked paprika before, look for it in the supermarket—it is sometimes called "pimenton." Use half chilli powder and half paprika, if you prefer.

SERVES 4

4 small baking potatoes, about 1 lb, cut into large dice
1 red onion, roughly chopped
1 red bell pepper, cored, seeded, and sliced
1 orange bell pepper, cored, seeded, and sliced
4 tomatoes, about 14 oz, roughly chopped
2 stems fresh rosemary
¾ teaspoon smoked paprika
3 tablespoons olive oil
4 eggs
Salt and ground black pepper

1. Bring a saucepan of water to a boil, add the potatoes, and cook for 4–5 minutes, until almost tender. Drain.

2. Put the onion, peppers, and tomatoes in a roasting pan, add the drained potatoes, and toss together. Tear the leaves from the rosemary stems over the vegetables then sprinkle with the paprika and salt and black pepper. Cover with aluminum foil and chill until ready to cook.

3. Preheat the oven to 200 400 F. Remove the foil cover from the roasting pan, drizzle the vegetables with the oil, and cook in the preheated oven for 35–40 minutes, stirring once, until the potatoes are golden.

4. Make four indentations among the vegetables and drop an egg into each space. Return the pan to the oven and cook for 5 minutes or until the eggs are done as you desire. Spoon onto plates and serve immediately.

STRATA

This colorful Italian-style polenta could easily be scaled up and cooked in a roasting pan if feeding a crowd. Vary the topping to suit your personal preferences, adding sliced mushrooms instead of salami for a vegetarian option.

SERVES 4

¾ cup coarse cornmeal (polenta)
4 tablespoons butter
½ cup freshly grated Parmesan
   cheese

TOPPING

1 small red onion, thinly sliced
½ yellow bell pepper, cored, seeded,
   and thinly sliced
½ green bell pepper, cored, seeded,
   and thinly sliced
1¾ cups cherry tomatoes, about
   7 oz, halved
12 small pitted black olives
2 oz sliced salami, halved
3 tablespoons olive oil
Basil leaves, if liked
Salt and ground black pepper

1. Line an 8-inch shallow, square baking pan with a large piece of nonstick parchment paper. Snip diagonally into the corners and press the paper into the pan so that it lines the bottom and sides.

2. Bring 2½ cups water to a boil in a large saucepan. Add the cornmeal and plenty of salt and black pepper and simmer for 3–4 minutes, stirring constantly, until the mixture is very thick. Stir in the butter and add two-thirds of the Parmesan.

3. Spoon the polenta into the lined pan and spread into an even layer. Let cool then cover with oiled plastic wrap or aluminum foil and chill for 2 hours or overnight.

4. Preheat the oven to 375°F. Put all the topping ingredients into a bowl with a little salt and black pepper and mix together. Remove the covering from the polenta, spoon over the topping, and bake in the preheated oven for 30 minutes or until the vegetables are tender and lightly browned.

5. Let stand for 5 minutes then lift the strata out of the pan, using the paper, and place on a cutting board. Sprinkle with the remaining Parmesan. Peel the paper away from the sides and cut the strata into four. Lift off the paper, transfer to serving plates with a spatula, and sprinkle with the remaining basil, if liked.

BOSTON BAKED BEANS

Real homemade baked beans are a revelation. Serve on toast for a light meal, or as an accompaniment to sausages.

SERVES 2

1 tablespoon vegetable oil
1 small red onion, finely chopped
2 celery ribs, finely chopped
1 garlic clove, crushed
¾ cup canned chopped tomatoes
⅔ cup vegetable stock
1 tablespoon dark soy sauce
1 tablespoon dark brown sugar
2 teaspoons Dijon mustard
1½ cups canned mixed beans,
    drained and rinsed
2 tablespoons chopped parsley,
    to serve

1. Heat the oil in a heavy saucepan. Add the onion and cook over low heat for 5 minutes or until softened. Add the celery and garlic and continue to cook for 1–2 minutes.

2. Add the tomatoes, stock, and soy sauce. Bring to a boil, then reduce the heat to a fast simmer and cook for about 15 minutes or until the sauce begins to thicken.

3. Add the sugar, mustard, and beans. Continue to cook for an additional 5 minutes, or until the beans are heated through. Stir in the chopped parsley and serve.

CHEESY CORNBREAD

An easy fork-together bread that bakes in around 30 minutes. Serve warm with ham and eggs, or toast any leftovers and top with broiled tomatoes.

SERVES 4–6

Oil for greasing
2 tablespoons butter
4 scallions, chopped
1 mild red chile, seeded and finely chopped
½ cup corn kernels, drained if canned, defrosted if frozen
¾ cup coarse cornmeal (polenta)
½ cup all-purpose flour
¼ cup grated Parmesan cheese
1 tablespoon superfine sugar
2 teaspoons cream of tartar
1 teaspoon baking soda
2 eggs
1¼ cups buttermilk
Salt and ground black pepper

1. Preheated the oven at 425°F. Brush the inside of an 8-inch springform pan with a little oil and line the bottom with a circle of nonstick parchment paper.

2. Melt the butter in a skillet, add the scallions and chile, and fry for 3–4 minutes until softened. Remove from the heat and stir in the corn.

3. Heat the springform pan in a preheated oven for 3–4 minutes.

4. Meanwhile, put the cornmeal, flour, and Parmesan into a mixing bowl. Add the sugar, cream of tartar, and baking soda and season with salt and black pepper. Mix together, then add the scallion mix, eggs, and buttermilk and fork together until just mixed.

5. Spoon the mixture into the hot pan, level the surface, and quickly return to the hot oven. Cook for 20–25 minutes, until the top is browned and the cornbread feels firm when pressed with a fingertip.

6. Loosen the edge of the bread, remove the pan and lining paper, and serve cut into thick slices.

PHILLY CHEESESTEAK

A popular dish from Philadelphia, it is reported this combination of thinly sliced steak and cheese was first created in the 1930s by Pat and Harry Oliveiri. The original version was topped with pizza sauce.

SERVES 2

¼ cup olive oil

½ red bell pepper, cored, seeded, and finely sliced

½ green bell pepper, cored, seeded, and finely sliced

1 small red onion, halved and finely sliced

10 oz rib-eye steak, finely sliced

1¼ cups sliced mushrooms, about 3 oz

1 garlic clove, chopped

3 oz provolone cheese, finely sliced

2 tablespoons Worcestershire or steak sauce

4 long slices of French bread

1 dill pickle, finely sliced (optional)

Salt and ground black pepper

1. Heat the olive oil in a skillet and add the bell peppers and onion. Cook over medium heat for 3–4 minutes, until just beginning to soften. Add the steak and continue cooking for 2–3 minutes before adding the mushrooms and garlic. Cook for an additional 3–4 minutes.

2. Reduce the heat to low and season well with salt and black pepper. Using two wooden spatulas form the steak mixture into two piles, roughly the size of the bread slices. Place the slices of cheese on top of each pile and let melt for 2 minutes.

3. Spread a little of the Worcestershire or steak sauce over two slices of bread and then very carefully lift the cheese-steak mixture onto the bread, again using two spatulas. Splash the remaining sauce over the mixture and arrange the pickle slices on top, if using.

4. Top with the two remaining bread slices to form two sandwiches and toast in a sandwich grill for 2–3 minutes, or according to the manufacturer's instructions, until the bread is crispy and the cheese is completely melted.

GRILLED ASPARAGUS WITH FETA AIOLI

This sophisticated dish is perfect for summer entertaining when asparagus is in season. To trim the asparagus spears, simply snap off the tough end of the stem. The point at which they snap easily is where the tough part ends and the tender part begins.

SERVES 6-8

4 bunches of asparagus, trimmed
3–4 tablespoons extra virgin olive oil, plus extra for tossing
7 oz feta cheese, crumbled
2 garlic cloves, crushed
1 tablespoon white wine vinegar
Salt and ground black pepper
Boiled new potatoes, to serve

1. Preheat a ridged grill pan or the broiler to hot.

2. Toss the trimmed asparagus in a little oil and season with salt and black pepper. Cook in the preheated ridged grill pan, or under the preheated hot broiler, for 3–4 minutes, turning when half done, until tender and charred.

3. Meanwhile, combine the feta, garlic, and vinegar in a blender or food processor and blend until smooth. Gradually blend in the remaining oil, a little at a time, until the sauce is thin, smooth, and glossy, then season with black pepper.

4. Transfer the aioli to a bowl and serve as a dip for the grilled asparagus. Serve with boiled new potatoes.

AKURI

These spicy Indian scrambled eggs make a wonderful "pick-me-up" breakfast, served with hot buttered toast or toasted ciabatta.

SERVES 4

1 tablespoon butter
1 small red onion, finely chopped
1 green chile, finely sliced
8 eggs, lightly beaten
1 tablespoon sour cream
1 tomato, skinned and finely chopped
1 tablespoon chopped cilantro
Sea salt
Buttered toast, to serve

1. Heat the butter in a large nonstick skillet, add the onion and chile, and cook for 2–3 minutes.

2. Add the eggs, sour cream, tomato, and cilantro. Season with sea salt and cook over a low heat, stirring frequently, for about 3–4 minutes, or until the eggs are lightly scrambled and set.

3. Serve hot with buttered toast.

TIP
To skin the tomato cut a cross into its top and place it in a large bowl. Pour over boiling water and let stand for 1minutes. Drain and leave to cool slightly, then peel off the skin.

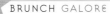

HERBY OMELET WITH AVOCADO

This sophisticated omelet topped with sour cream and smooth avocado makes an inspiring vegetarian brunch. The omelets are best eaten as soon as they are cooked, so make them one at a time and serve them as you work.

SERVES 4

12 eggs
¼ cup chopped mixed fresh herbs, such as chervil, chives, marjoram, parsley, and tarragon
4 tablespoons butter
¼ cup sour cream
1 avocado, peeled, pitted, and sliced
Salt and ground black pepper

1. Beat the eggs with the herbs and season with salt and black pepper. Melt a quarter of the butter in an omelet pan or small skillet, then swirl in a quarter of the egg mixture. Fork over the omelet so that it cooks evenly.

2. As soon as it is set on the bottom (but still a little runny in the middle) carefully slide the omelet onto a warmed serving plate, folding it in half as you do so.

3. Repeat with the remaining mixture to make three more omelets. Serve the omelets as soon as they are cooked, topped with sour cream and sliced avocado.

SMOKED SALMON & TARAMA TIMBALES

The combination of smoked salmon and taramasalata spiked with a dash of Tabasco sauce and a touch of cayenne pepper makes an excellent appetizer for a brunch party.

SERVES 4

1 tablespoon sunflower oil
6 oz smoked salmon, thinly sliced
6 oz taramasalata
⅔ cup cream cheese
Dash of Tabasco sauce
Juice of ½ lemon
Pinch of cayenne pepper
TO GARNISH
Lemon wedges
Argula
Loose lettuce leaves

1. Grease four timbale molds with the sunflower oil. Line the molds with smoked salmon. Reserve a few slices to cover the tops of the molds once they are filled, and chop any leftover salmon into small pieces.

2. Put the taramasalata, cream cheese, Tabasco sauce, lemon juice, and cayenne pepper in a bowl and mix. Add any chopped leftover salmon.

3. Divide the mixture between the prepared molds. Level the tops, cover with the reserved smoked salmon, and chill well for 2–3 hours.

4. To serve, carefully turn the timbales out of the molds and garnish with lemon wedges, argula, and lettuce leaves.

SUPER CLUB WITH GRAIN MUSTARD

Made with multigrain bread, this sandwich is just as delicious made with white bread if you have a few more fussy eaters to satisfy.

SERVES 2

¼ cup mayonnaise

2 tablespoons whole-grain mustard

4 slices of multigrain bread

2 slices of honey-roast ham

3 oz deli-style turkey, in wafer-thin slices

3 oz sharp cheddar cheese, finely sliced

1 large beefsteak tomato, sliced

½ small red onion, finely sliced

6 slices of cooked bacon

6 gherkin pickles, finely sliced (optional)

2 tablespoons chopped chives

1. Combine the mayonnaise and mustard in a small bowl and spread the mixture over one side of each slice of bread.

2. Arrange the ham slices on two slices of bread, followed by the sliced turkey. Top with the cheddar and tomato and sprinkle with the onion. Top with the bacon and sliced pickles, if using, then sprinkle the chives over the filling and cover with the remaining two slices of bread.

3. Toast in a sandwich grill for 3–4 minutes, or according to the manufacturer's instructions, until the filling is hot and melting and the bread is golden. Serve immediately with the remaining mayonnaise and mustard sauce—and plenty of napkins!

SPICED FRIES WITH SMOKY TOMATO SALSA

This is a great choice for anyone who loves fries but avoids them because of their high fat content. Here, the potato wedges are coated with spices and egg white and then baked, rather than fried. The exterior is crisp but the center soft.

SERVES 8

Olive oil spray, for greasing
8 potatoes, about 5 oz each
2 egg whites
1 teaspoon ground paprika
Pinch of cayenne pepper
Salt and ground black pepper

SMOKY TOMATO SALSA
4 ripe tomatoes
2 garlic cloves, unpeeled
1 red onion, cut into wedges
¼ cup extra virgin olive oil
1 tablespoon lime juice
2 tablespoons chopped cilantro

1. Preheat the oven to 400°F and preheat the broiler to hot. Line a baking sheet with nonstick parchment paper sprayed with olive oil.

2. Cut the potatoes into chunky wedges and place in a bowl. Lightly beat the egg whites until frothy and stir into the potato wedges so they are evenly coated. Add the spices and plenty of salt and black pepper and toss again to lightly coat the wedges with seasoning.

3. Arrange the wedges in a single layer on the prepared baking sheet and cook them in a preheated oven for about 30 minutes, turning a couple of times, until roasted and golden.

4. To make the salsa, cook the tomatoes under the preheated broiler, turning, for 1–2 minutes, until the skin chars and blisters. Skewer the garlic cloves and onion wedges on a long metal skewer and broil for 3–4 minutes on each side, until they are charred and softened.

5. Peel, seed, and finely chop the tomatoes, peel and crush the garlic, and finely chop the onion. Place in a bowl and add the remaining ingredients. Season with salt and black pepper and serve with the potato wedges.

SPANISH FRITTATA

Brimming with eggs, potato, and chorizo, the Spanish frittata is a substantial dish, and is delicious served with salad and crusty bread.

SERVES 4

¼ cup olive oil

1 small Bermuda onion, sliced

½ cup cold, cooked potatoes, thickly sliced, about 4 oz

2 oz finely sliced chorizo sausage, shredded (optional)

3 oz roasted red bell peppers from a jar, drained and cut into strips

1 garlic clove, crushed

½ teaspoon paprika

3 tablespoons roughly chopped flat-leaf parsley

2 teaspoons chopped fresh marjoram, plus extra to garnish

3 large eggs, lightly beaten

½ cup shredded cheddar cheese

Salt and ground black pepper

1. Preheat the boiler and heat the olive oil in a small ovenproof skillet. Add the onion and fry over medium heat until it is softened and golden, then add the potato and fry until hot and golden. Add the chorizo, if using, red bell peppers, garlic, paprika, and herbs, and stir until combined.

2. Add the eggs and season with salt and black pepper. Let the mixture cook until the eggs are set, stirring occasionally to prevent them from sticking to the skillet.

3. Sprinkle the cheddar over the frittata, then place the skillet under the preheated broiler until the cheese is melted and bubbling. Remove and let cool.

4. Once the frittata is cool enough to handle, cut it into quarters. Sprinkle with fresh marjoram to garnish.

BLUE CHEESE & WALNUT SCONES

Here is a good way to use up that wedge of blue cheese that's been in the refrigerator a little too long. These rustic scones, a variation of biscuits, are rolled out thickly then cut into wedges, but they could also be cut into small rounds, like biscuits, and cooked for 12–15 minutes. Serve warm with just a little butter, or top with wafer thin ham or even folds of smoked salmon.

SERVES 4–6

Oil, for greasing
2½ cups self-rising flour
4 tablespoons butter, diced
5 oz blue cheese, such as Stilton,
    Danish blue, or St. Agur, rind
    removed, diced
½ cup walnuts, roughly chopped
1 egg, beaten
About ¾ cup milk
Salt and ground black pepper

1. Preheat the oven to 400°F and grease a baking sheet with a little oil.

2. Put the flour into a large bowl with some salt and black pepper. Add the butter and blend until it forms fine crumbs, then stir in the cheese and nuts.

3. Pour in all but 1 tablespoon of the beaten egg, then gradually mix in enough milk to make a soft but not sticky dough, adjusting with extra milk, if needed.

4. Knead briefly on a lightly floured surface, then roll out thickly into a rough circle about 7 inches across. Cut into eight wedges.

5. Transfer the wedges to the oiled baking sheet, arranging as a circle but allowing a little space between each. Brush the tops with the remaining egg and cook in the preheated oven for about 20 minutes, until well risen. Serve the scones warm, split, and spread with a little butter.

HUSH PUPPIES

Quick and easy to fork together these hush puppies are delicious. Serve with baked beans and broiled sausages if you are feeling hungry, or just dunk into a little ketchup if you are not so ravenous.

SERVES 4-6

1⅔ cups coarse cornmeal
1 cup all-purpose flour
2 teaspoons baking powder
1 teaspoon mustard powder
¼ teaspoon salt
¼ teaspoon cayenne pepper
1 cup coarsely shredded cheddar
   cheese, plus extra to serve
½ cup corn kernels, drained if canned,
   defrosted if frozen
6 scallions, finely chopped
1⅓ cups blonde beer
Sunflower oil for deep-frying

1. Put the cornmeal, flour, baking powder, mustard, salt, and cayenne pepper into a bowl and stir together with a fork. Add the cheese, corn, and scallions, then gradually mix in enough beer until the batter is a soft dropping consistency.

2. Pour the oil into a large saucepan and heat to 340°F using a kitchen thermometer, or until a little of the corn mixture bubbles immediately around the edges and floats when added to the hot oil.

3. Drop 5 or 6 large spoonfuls of the mixture carefully into the oil, each slightly spaced apart, and cook for 3–4 minutes, until they have risen to the surface and turned golden brown. Lift out of the oil with a draining spoon and put onto a plate lined with paper towels.

4. Continue cooking the corn mixture in batches, making sure that you do not overload the pan and keeping a watchful eye that the temperature of the oil stays between 325 and 340°F. Do not leave the pan unattended while the hush puppies are cooking.

5. Transfer the hush puppies to a fresh plate lined with more paper towels and sprinkle them with a little more grated cheese. Serve hot.

PANCAKES

KARTOFFELPUFFER

Inspired by classic German potato cakes, these are made with grated onion and potato and are like a cross between a drop biscuit and a rosti.

SERVES 4

APPLE COMPOTE
3 apples
2 tablespoons butter
2 tablespoons sherry or cider vinegar
2 tablespoons superfine sugar
2 tablespoons water

PANCAKES
6 medium potatoes, about 1½ lb
1 onion
1 cup all-purpose flour
1 teaspoon baking powder
2 eggs
3–4 tablespoons sunflower oil
Salt and ground black pepper

TO SERVE
1 cup sour cream
Coarsely ground black pepper
4 sweet-sour cucumbers, sliced
Pastrami or broiled bacon

1. To make the apple compote, core and thickly slice the apples. Melt the butter in a skillet, add the apples, and fry for 3 minutes, stirring, until just beginning to brown. Add the vinegar, sugar, and water and cook for 4–5 minutes, stirring, until the apples are hot and the liquid syrupy.

2. Meanwhile, coarsely grate the potatoes and onion and pat dry with paper towels.

3. Put the flour, baking powder, and some salt and black pepper into a bowl. Add the potatoes, onion, and eggs and mix together.

4. Heat a little oil in a large nonstick skillet and drop large spoonfuls of the potato mixture into the skillet, leaving room between the spoonfuls and flattening them slightly with the back of the spoon. Cook over medium heat until the undersides are golden. Turn over and continue to cook until the potato is tender and the second side browned.

5. Remove the pancakes from the skillet and keep hot while you cook the remaining mixture in the same way until you have eight pancakes.

6. To serve, arrange two pancakes on each serving plate. Top with spoonfuls of sour cream, apple compote, and a sprinkling of coarsely ground pepper. Next to the pancakes arrange some cucumbers and thickly sliced pastrami or bacon. Serve immediately.

HAZELNUT CREPES WITH ROAST PEARS

SERVES 4

CREPES

Generous ½ cup hazelnuts
⅔ cup all-purpose flour
1 egg plus 1 egg yolk
1¼ cups milk
Sunflower oil for frying
Sour cream or whipped cream,
   to serve

ROAST PEARS

4 just ripe pears, about 1½ lb,
   cored and thickly sliced
2 tablespoons butter
2 tablespoons superfine sugar

CHEAT'S CHOCOLATE SAUCE

½ cup chocolate spread
½ cup milk

1. Preheat the oven to 375°F and preheat the boiler. Put the hazelnuts in a broiler pan and toast under the preheated broiler until golden. Cool slightly, then roughly chop one-third and reserve for decoration. Grind the rest in a blender or food processor until almost powder.

2. To make the crepes, sift the flour into a bowl and add the ground hazelnuts, whole egg, and egg yolk. Gradually beat in the milk to form a smooth batter. Let stand for 15 minutes.

3. Meanwhile, put the pears into a roasting pan, dot with the butter, and sprinkle with the sugar. Bake in the preheated oven for 15 minutes until just beginning to brown.

4. Put the sauce ingredients into a small saucepan and heat gently, until smooth.

5. Heat a little oil in a 7-inch skillet. Pour the excess into a cup then pour 2–3 tablespoons of the batter into the skillet, tilting the skillet to coat it evenly. Cook until the underside is golden brown. Turn over with a spatula, or flip, and cook the second side. Slide out of the skillet onto a plate and keep hot. Repeat with the remaining batter, oiling the pan as needed, until you have eight thin crepes.

6. Divide the pears between the crepes, fold in half, and transfer to serving plates. Drizzle the sauce over, sprinkle with the reserved chopped hazelnuts, and serve with spoonfuls of sour cream or whipped cream.

BUTTERMILK PANCAKES

Light, fluffy, and delicious, these thick pancakes are best served straight from the skillet topped with a little butter and jelly or a spoonful of lemon curd. If you don't have any buttermilk, then use the amount of low-fat plain yogurt mixed with half the amount of milk instead.

SERVES 4

1½ cups all-purpose flour
1 teaspoon baking powder
½ teaspoon baking soda
2 eggs, separated
1 cup plus 3 tablespoons buttermilk
Sunflower oil for frying
Butter and jelly, to serve

1. Sift the flour, baking powder, and baking soda into a bowl. Put the egg whites into a medium bowl and beat until they form soft peaks.

2. Add the egg yolks and buttermilk to the flour and beat together until smooth. With a large spoon, fold in the egg whites.

3. Heat a large nonstick skillet or griddle, then wipe with a piece of folded paper towel moistened with a little oil. Drop large spoonfuls of the pancake mixture into the skillet, leaving space between to let them to expand. Cook over medium heat until the undersides are golden and the tops are bubbling. Turn over and cook the second side in the same way until cooked through to the center. Lift out of the pan and keep hot in a folded dish towel.

4. Continue oiling the skillet and frying spoonfuls of the mixture until used up.

5. Serve the pancakes warm with a little butter and spoonfuls of jelly.

SOUFFLÉ STRAWBERRY PANCAKES

SERVES 4

¾ cup all-purpose flour
Grated zest of 1 lemon, plus extra
   to decorate
2 eggs plus 2 egg whites
1 cup milk
¼ cup superfine sugar
4 tablespoons butter
Sifted confectioners' sugar,
   for dusting
Whole-milk yogurt, to serve
Fresh mint leaves, to decorate

TOPPING

3 cups strawberries, sliced
¼ cup strawberry jelly
Juice of 1 lemon

1. Sift the flour into a bowl and add the lemon zest. Separate the whole eggs and add the whites to the extra whites. Add the yolks to the flour and gradually beat in the milk to form a smooth batter. Allow to stand for 15 minutes.

2. Preheat the broiler. For the topping, put the strawberries, jelly, and lemon juice into a saucepan and then heat gently for 4–5 minutes, until the jelly has melted and the strawberries are warmed through.

3. Beat the egg whites to form soft moist peaks, then gradually beat in the superfine sugar a little at a time until thick and glossy. Fold a large spoonful of the egg whites into the pancake batter to loosen it slightly, then fold in the rest of the egg whites.

4. Heat a quarter of the butter in an 7-inch skillet. Add a quarter of the pancake batter and fry over medium heat for 2–3 minutes, until the underside of the pancake is golden. Transfer to the broiler and cook until the top is golden and the pancake just cooked through.

5. Loosen the edges with a spatula, then quickly slide the pancake out onto a large plate. Top with quarter of the strawberries and fold the pancake in half. Transfer to a serving plate, dust with confectioners' sugar, and serve with spoonfuls of yogurt. Decorate with mint and lemon zest. Serve immediately.

6. Wipe the inside of the pan with paper towels, then repeat steps 4 and 5 using the remaining batter.

BUCKWHEAT SALMON CREPES

SERVES 4

CREPES
¾ cup buckwheat flour
2 eggs
1 tablespoon olive oil
1¼ cups milk
Sunflower oil for frying

FILLING
2 salmon fillets, about 12 oz
1¼ cups milk
1 bay leaf
2 tablespoons butter
¼ cup all-purpose flour
2 cups baby leaf spinach
2 scallions, chopped
Grated nutmeg
½ cup freshly grated Parmesan
   cheese
Salt and ground black pepper

1. To make the crepes, put the flour into a mixing bowl with a little salt. Add the eggs and oil and gradually beat in the milk until smooth. Set aside while making the filling.

2. Put the salmon into a saucepan, pour over the milk, and add the bay leaf and a little salt and black pepper. Bring the milk to a boil, cover, and simmer for 8 minutes, until the salmon is cooked and flakes easily when pressed in the center with a knife.

3. In a separate saucepan, melt the butter, stir in the flour, then gradually mix in the milk from cooking the salmon. Bring the sauce to a boil, stirring until thickened and smooth. Add the spinach, scallions, a little nutmeg, and half the Parmesan. Cook for 2 minutes until the spinach has just wilted.

4. Remove the skin from the salmon and flake the fish into large pieces, discarding any bones. Stir the salmon into the sauce. Cover and keep hot.

5. To make the pancakes, heat a little oil in the bottom of a large nonstick skillet. Pour the excess oil into a cup, then spoon about one-quarter of the batter into the pan. Cook until lightly browned on the underside, then loosen the pancake and turn over with a spatula. Cook the second side, then slide out of the pan onto a plate. Repeat until four pancakes have been made.

6. Reheat the sauce, if necessary. Put each pancake onto a serving plate, divide the sauce among them, then fold the pancake edges over like a parcel. Sprinkle with the remaining Parmesan and serve immediately.

PARSLEY POTATO HOT CAKES WITH BACON

SERVES 4–6

1 generous cup leftover, cooked mashed potato

2 cups all-purpose flour, plus extra for dusting

1 teaspoon baking soda

¼ cup chopped parsley

⅔ cup low-fat plain yogurt or buttermilk

1 egg

1–2 tablespoons milk

2 tablespoons butter, plus extra for spreading

2–3 tablespoons sunflower oil

12 slices of bacon, about 8 oz

24 cherry tomatoes, halved

2 stems of fresh rosemary

3 tablespoons maple syrup

Salt and ground black pepper

1. Preheat the oven to 400°F and preheat the broiler.

2. Put the mashed potato, flour, and baking soda into a bowl with plenty of salt and black pepper. Stir in the parsley, then add the yogurt or buttermilk, egg, and enough milk to mix to a soft but not sticky dough.

3. Knead the dough briefly on a well-floured surface, then lightly roll out to a thickness of ¾ inch. Stamp out circles with a 2-inch plain cutter. Reroll the trimmings and continue until all the dough has been shaped.

4. Heat the butter and oil in a large skillet. Add the potato cakes (cook in batches, if necessary) and fry over medium heat until the undersides are golden. Turn over and cook the other side in the same way. If the skillet is ovenproof put it straight into the preheated oven. Alternatively, transfer the cakes to a baking sheet. Cook for 5–10 minutes, until the cakes are cooked through.

5. Meanwhile, line the broiler rack with aluminum foil and arrange the bacon and tomatoes on top. Tear the leaves from the rosemary, chop, and sprinkle over the tomatoes with a little salt and black pepper. Broil until the bacon is almost cooked, then drizzle with the maple syrup and continue to cook until the fat is golden.

6. To serve, halve the potato cakes, spread with a little butter, and fill with pieces of bacon and halved tomatoes. Arrange on a large platter and serve immediately.

ZUCCHINI & PEA GRIDDLE CAKES

SERVES 4

CHILI RELISH

1 tablespoon sunflower oil

½ red onion, finely chopped

1 red bell pepper, cored, seeded and chopped

1–2 large mild chiles, to taste, seeded and finely chopped

4 tomatoes, skinned if liked, chopped

¼ cup superfine sugar

2 tablespoons red wine vinegar

Salt and ground black pepper

PANCAKES

1 medium zucchini, about 10 oz, coarsely grated

1⅓ cups frozen peas, defrosted and roughly mashed

4 scallions, chopped

¼ cup chopped fresh mint

1 cup all-purpose flour

1 egg

3–4 tablespoons sunflower oil

TO SERVE

⅔ cup whole-milk yogurt

6-oz canned white crabmeat, drained and flaked

Extra mint leaves, to garnish

1. To make the relish, heat the oil in a medium saucepan and add the onion, bell pepper, and chiles. Fry for 5 minutes, until softened, then stir in the tomatoes, sugar, vinegar, and a little salt and black pepper. Simmer gently for 15 minutes, stirring occasionally, until thick.

2. To make the pancakes, put the zucchini, peas, scallions, and mint into a mixing bowl. Add the flour, egg, and a little salt and black pepper and mix together.

3. Heat a little of the oil in a large skillet. When hot, drop large spoonfuls of the mixture into the skillet, then flatten each mound slightly and cook until the underside is golden brown. Turn over with a spatula and cook the second side in the same way.

4. Transfer the pancakes to a plate and keep hot while cooking the remaining mixture. You should end up with about 12 pancakes.

5. To serve, arrange two or three pancakes on each serving plate and top with a spoonful of yogurt, some chili relish and the crabmeat. Sprinkle with mint leaves, if liked. Serve immediately.

GUZLEME

These Turkish pancakes are rolled out thinly and resemble a soft flour tortilla more than a true pancake. Although they can be eaten cold, they are very tasty eaten as soon as they have been shaped.

SERVES 4

1 cup bread flour
Salt
1 tablespoon olive oil, plus extra
    for frying
About ⅓ cup warm water
A few cherry tomatoes or tomato
    salad, to serve
FILLING
4 cups baby leaf spinach
6 scallions, finely chopped
1–2 garlic cloves, finely chopped
6 oz feta cheese, drained and
    crumbled
About ¼ teaspoon crushed red
    pepper (dried chile flakes)

1. To make the pancakes, put the flour and a little salt into a bowl. Add the oil and mix in enough warm water to make a soft but not sticky dough. Knead well on a lightly floured surface, then wrap in a plastic bag and let rest for 15 minutes.

2. Cut the dough into four and roll each piece into a rough circle, about 8 inches in diameter.

3. Heat a little oil in a large skillet, then pour off the excess into a cup. Add one of the pancakes and fry until the underside is blistered and golden brown.

4. Turn over with a spatula, then sprinkle with a quarter of the spinach, scallions, and feta and a little crushed pepper to taste. Cook until the second side is golden and the spinach has just wilted.

5. Slide the pancake out of the skillet onto a square of nonstick parchment paper. Roll up tightly. Cook the remaining pancakes in the same way, oiling the pan as needed.

6. Cut each pancake into three and serve warm, or cold, with a few cherry tomatoes or tomato salad.

APPLE & RAISIN PANCAKES

Made with ingredients that you will already have in store, these delicious thick pancakes taste just as good for an afternoon snack as for brunch.

SERVES 4

CINNAMON BUTTER

4 tablespoons butter, at room temperature
3 tablespoons light brown sugar
¼ teaspoon ground cinnamon

PANCAKES

1½ cups all-purpose flour
1 teaspoon baking powder
½ teaspoon baking soda
2 tablespoons light brown sugar
2 eggs, separated
1 large apple, cored and coarsely grated (peel left on)
⅔ cup plain yogurt
2 tablespoons milk
⅓ cup golden raisins
Sunflower oil for frying

1. Beat all the ingredients for the cinnamon butter together and spoon into a small dish.

2. Sift the flour, baking powder, and baking soda into a bowl, then stir in the sugar. Beat the egg whites in a separate bowl, until they form moist peaks.

3. Add the egg yolks, grated apple, yogurt, and milk to the flour mixture and stir together. Stir in the golden raisins, followed by 1 tablespoon of the egg white to loosen the mixture. Gently fold in the remaining egg white.

4. Heat a large skillet or griddle, then wipe with a folded piece of paper towel moistened with oil. Add large spoonfuls of the pancake mixture to the skillet, leaving space between them.

5. Cook over medium heat for 2–3 minutes, until the underside of each pancake is golden and the surface is beginning to bubble. Turn over with a spatula and cook the second side. Lift the cooked pancakes out of the skillet and keep hot in a folded dish towel.

6. Continue oiling the skillet and frying spoonfuls of the mixture until used up. Serve the pancakes spread with a little of the cinnamon butter.

WHOLE-WHEAT CREPES WITH LEMON CREAM

Don't keep that jar of lemon curd just for spreading on toast. When added to whipped cream it makes an easy cheat's filling that goes really well with the exotic perfume of freshly spooned passion fruit.

SERVES 4

CREPES

¾ cup whole-wheat flour

2 eggs

1 tablespoon sunflower oil, plus
   extra for frying

1¼ cups milk

4 passion fruit

¾ cup raspberries, to serve

FILLING

3 tablespoons lemon curd

¾ cup heavy (double) cream

1. To make the crepes, put the flour into a mixing bowl. Add the eggs and oil, then gradually beat in the milk until smooth. Let stand for 15 minutes.

2. For the filling, put the lemon curd into a bowl, add the cream, and beat together until thick and the cream forms soft peaks.

3. Heat a little oil in a small skillet, then pour off the excess into a cup. Pour just enough batter into the skillet to thinly coat the bottom. Cook until the underside is golden, then turn over with a spatula and cook the second side. Slide the crepe out onto a plate. Repeat, oiling the pan as needed, until you have at least eight crepes.

4. Spoon a little lemon cream onto each crepe, then fold in hald and arrange two on each serving plate. Cut the passion fruit in half and scoop the seeds over the crepes using a teaspoon. Sprinkle over the raspberries, then serve immediately.

CARIBBEAN GINGERED DROP BISCUITS

Popular in Jamaican cuisine, allspice is more commonly used in its ground form. The berries taste like a mixture of cloves, cinnamon, and nutmeg and add a delicate perfume to this dish.

SERVES 4

¼ cup light brown sugar
10 allspice berries, roughly crushed
Grated zest and juice of 1 lime
3 bananas, thickly sliced
Plain yogurt, to serve
Extra grated lime zest, to decorate
DROP BISCUITS
1¼ cups self-rising flour
½ teaspoon baking powder
2 tablespoons light brown sugar
4 pieces drained preserved ginger,
   finely chopped
2 eggs
⅔ cup milk
Sunflower oil, for frying

1. Put the sugar, allspice berries, lime zest and juice, and 2 tablespoons water into a small saucepan. Heat gently until the sugar has dissolved, then simmer for 2–3 minutes. Add the bananas, toss in the syrup, then take off the heat.

2. To make the drop biscuits, sift the flour and baking powder into a mixing bowl. Stir in the sugar and ginger, then add the eggs. Gradually beat in the milk until the mixture is smooth.

3. Heat a large skillet or griddle and wipe with a piece of folded paper towel moistened with oil. Drop large spoonfuls of the batter into the skillet and cook until the underside is golden and bubbles appear on the surface. Turn over with a spatula and cook until the biscuits are golden on both sides and cooked through. Lift out of the skillet and keep warm in a folded dish towel. Continue cooking the rest of the batter in the same way.

4. Reheat the bananas if necessary. Divide the drop biscuits among serving plates and top with spoonfuls of yogurt and the warm bananas. Sprinkle with extra lime zest, if liked, and serve immediately.

RAISIN & CREAM CHEESE BLINTZ

SERVES 4

¾ cup all-purpose flour

2 eggs

1 tablespoon sunflower oil, plus extra
   for frying

1 cup milk

2 tablespoons butter

Sifted confectioners' sugar,
   for dusting

FILLING

1 cup cream cheese

2 tablespoons wheat germ

⅓ cup raisins

2 tablespoons superfine sugar

Grated zest of 1 orange

APRICOT SAUCE

½ cup apricot jelly

Juice of 1 orange

1. Sift the flour into a bowl and add a whole egg, an egg yolk (reserving the white), and the oil. Gradually beat in the milk until smooth. Let stand for 15 minutes.

2. Heat a little oil in a 7-inch skillet, then pour off the excess into a cup. Pour 2–3 tablespoons of the batter into the skillet, tilt to coat evenly, and cook until the underside is golden. Turn over with a spatula, or flip, and cook the second side. Slide the pancake out of the skillet onto a plate. Repeat with the remaining batter until you have made eight thin pancakes.

3. Put all the filling ingredients into a second bowl and beat together until smooth. Divide among the pancakes, spreading into a thick circle over the center. Brush the edges with the reserved egg white. Fold in the sides, then fold the top edge down and the bottom edge up so that the filling is completely covered and you have a square parcel. Put seam side downward on a baking sheet, cover with plastic wrap, and chill overnight if liked.

4. Warm the jelly and orange juice together in a small saucepan, or microwave in a bowl for 30 seconds. Stir and cook a little longer, if needed.

5. Heat the butter in a large skillet, add the blintz, and fry on both sides until hot through—if using a small skillet you may need to heat the blintz in batches. Transfer to serving plates, dust with sifted confectioners' sugar, and spoon the warm sauce around.

SOUR CREAM PANCAKES WITH SPICED APRICOTS

These light, velvety thick pancakes are topped with poached dried apricots scented with crushed cardamom pods. Fresh apricots can be used when in season: use 1 lb apricots and reduce the quantity of water by one-third.

SERVES 6

SPICED APRICOTS
1½ cups dried apricots, halved
2 tablespoons honey
1 cup water
Juice of 1 lemon
10 cardamom pods, roughly crushed
PANCAKES
1¼ cups self-rising flour
1 teaspoon baking powder
2 tablespoons superfine sugar
2 eggs
⅔ cup sour cream, plus extra to serve
¼ cup milk
3–4 tablespoons sunflower oil

1. Put all the ingredients for the spiced apricots into a saucepan, including the green cardamom pods as well as the tiny black seeds. Cook over medium heat for 5 minutes, until the apricots are plumped up and the liquid is syrupy.

2. For the pancakes, sift the flour and baking powder into a mixing bowl. Add the sugar followed by the eggs, sour cream, and milk and beat to a thick batter.

3. Heat a large skillet or griddle and wipe with a piece of folded paper towel moistened with oil. Drop large spoonfuls of the mixture into the skillet and cook until the undersides are golden and the tops are bubbling. Turn over with a spatula and cook the second sides in the same way until cooked through to the center. Lift out of the skillet and keep hot in a folded dish towel. Continue oiling the skillet and frying spoonfuls of the mixture until used up.

4. Serve the pancakes warm with spoonfuls of the spiced apricots and a little extra sour cream.

CARAMELIZED ONION & CHEESE CREPES

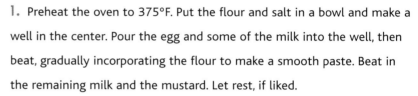

SERVES 4

1¼ cups whole-wheat flour
Pinch of salt
1 egg, lightly beaten
1¼ cups milk
1 tablespoon mustard
Sunflower oil for frying
FILLING
3 tablespoons butter
3 onions, thinly sliced
2 teaspoons superfine sugar
A few thyme sprigs
2 cups shredded Emmental or
    Gruyère cheese, about 8 oz, grated
Salt and ground black pepper

1. Preheat the oven to 375°F. Put the flour and salt in a bowl and make a well in the center. Pour the egg and some of the milk into the well, then beat, gradually incorporating the flour to make a smooth paste. Beat in the remaining milk and the mustard. Let rest, if liked.

2. Heat a little oil in a 7-inch crepe pan or heavy skillet until it starts to smoke, then pour off the excess into a cup. Pour a quarter of the batter into the pan, tilting it until the bottom is coated with a thin layer. Cook for 1–2 minutes, until the underside begins to turn golden.

3. Turn the crepe with a spatula. Cook for an additional 30–45 seconds, until it is golden on the second side. Repeat with the remaining batter, oiling the pan as necessary, to make three more crepes.

4. To make the filling, melt the butter in a heavy saucepan and sauté the onions with the sugar for about 8–10 minutes, until they are a deep golden color and caramelized. Tear the thyme leaves off the stems and add them to the pan with salt and plenty of black pepper.

5. Set aside ¼ cup of the cheese and sprinkle the remainder over the crepes. Arrange a quarter of the sautéed onions on one half of a crepe, then fold over and place in a lightly greased, shallow baking dish. Repeat for the remaining crepes.

6. Sprinkle with the reserved cheese and bake in the preheated oven for about 15 minutes, until the cheese has melted. Serve warm.

CORNMEAL PANCAKES WITH CHORIZO

These rustic, Spanish-style pancakes can be difficult to roll out. If they fall apart as you lift them off the plastic wrap, simply press back into a smaller, thicker round and flatten slightly with the back of a spatula once in the skillet.

SERVES 4

1½ cups fine cornmeal
1 egg
About 1 cup water
Sunflower oil for frying
Salt and ground black pepper
TOPPING
1 tablespoon olive oil
1 red onion, roughly chopped
5 oz chorizo in one piece, skinned
  and diced
1 yellow bell pepper, cored, seeded,
  and diced
4 plum tomatoes, diced
4 eggs
Chopped flat-leaf parsley, to garnish

1. Put the cornmeal into a bowl and season with a little salt and pepper. Add the egg, then mix in enough water to form a soft dough that you can squeeze together. Place in a plastic bag and let rest for 15–20 minutes.

2. To make the topping, heat the olive oil in a skillet, add the onion, and fry for 5 minutes, stirring until softened. Add the chorizo, yellow pepper, and tomatoes and fry, stirring, for another 5 minutes.

3. Cut the dough into four. Roll each piece between two sheets of plastic wrap into a rough circle, about 4 inches across.

4. Heat a little sunflower oil in a second large skillet and, using a spatula, lift the pancakes into the skillet (you will probably need to cook them in two batches). Fry for 3–4 minutes, turning once, until golden brown on both sides. Remove from the skillet and keep hot.

5. Add a little more oil to the skillet and fry the eggs until cooked to your liking. Reheat the chorizo mixture. Transfer the cornmeal pancakes to serving plates, then top with the chorizo mix and a well-drained fried egg. Garnish with chopped parsley and serve immediately.

PIROSHKIS

SERVES 4

PANCAKES
¾ cup all-purpose flour
2 eggs
1 tablespoon sunflower oil, plus extra
    for frying
1 cup milk
2 tablespoons butter
FILLING
1 generous cup cream cheese
2 egg yolks
4 scallions or ½ onion, finely chopped
SALAD
2 tablespoons olive oil
¼ cup walnut pieces
2 teaspoons cider vinegar
1¼ cups mixed salad greens
Salt and ground black pepper

1. First make the pancakes. Sift the flour into a bowl, season with salt and pepper, and add one whole egg, one egg yolk (reserving the white), and the oil. Gradually beat in the milk until smooth. Let stand for 15 minutes.

2. Heat a little oil in a 7-inch skillet, then pour the excess into a cup. Pour 2–3 tablespoons of the batter into the skillet, tilt to coat evenly, and cook until golden on the underside. Turn over with a spatula and cook the second side. Slide the pancake out of the skillet onto a plate.

3. Repeat with the remaining batter until you have made eight thin pancakes and all the batter has been used.

4. Beat the filling ingredients with some salt and black pepper in a bowl. Divide among the pancakes, spreading into a thick circle over the center. Brush the edges with the reserved egg white, then fold the sides in and roll the pancake to form a cylinder-shape parcel. Put seam side downward on a baking sheet, cover with plastic wrap, and chill overnight, if liked.

5. About 15 minutes before serving, heat the oil for the salad in a small pan, add the walnuts, and fry for 2–3 minutes, until lightly browned. Remove from the heat, add the vinegar and a little salt and black pepper, and set aside.

6. Heat the butter in a large skillet and add the piroshkis. Fry, turning several times, until heated through. Toss the salad greens with the warm walnut dressing. Arrange two piroshkis on each serving plate and garnish with the salad. Serve immediately.

VANILLA & BANANA PANCAKES

SERVES 4

VANILLA MAPLE BUTTER
¼ lb (1 stick) unsalted butter, softened
1½ teaspoons vanilla extract
2 tablespoons confectioners' sugar
3 teaspoons pure maple syrup

PANCAKES
2 bananas
1 teaspoon vanilla extract
1 cup self-rising flour
1 teaspoon baking powder
1 tablespoon superfine sugar
1 egg
⅓ cup milk
1 tablespoon butter, melted
Sunflower oil for frying

1. Put the butter, vanilla extract, and sugar in a small bowl and beat with a handheld electric beater until the ingredients are combined.

2. Gradually blend in the maple syrup, a little at a time, until the mixture is soft and smooth. Transfer to a small serving dish, cover, and chill until required. The butter can be kept in the refrigerator for up to a week.

3. For the pancakes, mash the bananas with the vanilla extract to make a puree. Sift the flour and baking powder into a bowl and stir in the sugar.

4. Beat the egg with the milk and melted butter, then beat into the dry ingredients until smooth. Stir in the banana puree.

5. Heat a large skillet or griddle and wipe with a piece of folded paper towel moistened with oil. Drop in large spoonfuls of the batter, spacing them well apart. (You'll probably be able to cook three or four pancakes at a time.) Cook for about 3 minutes, until bubbles appear on the surface and the undersides are golden. Turn the pancakes with a spatula and cook for an additional 1–2 minutes.

6. Lift out of the skillet and keep warm in a folded dish towel while cooking the remainder. Serve hot with the vanilla maple butter.

SUMMER BERRY BLINTZ

SERVES 4

¾ cup all-purpose flour
2 eggs
1 tablespoon sunflower oil, plus
  extra for frying
1 cup milk
2 tablespoons butter
Sifted confectioners' sugar,
  for dusting

FILLING
¾ cup cream cheese
2 tablespoons wheat germ
3 tablespoons superfine sugar
Grated zest of 1 lemon
1 egg yolk

BERRY COMPOTE
2 cups frozen mixed summer berries
2 tablespoons superfine sugar
Juice of 1 lemon

1. Sift the flour into a bowl. Add one whole egg, one egg yolk (reserving the white), and the oil, then gradually beat in the milk until smooth. Let stand for 15 minutes.

2. Heat a little oil in a 7-inch skillet, then pour off the excess into a cup. Pour 2–3 tablespoons of the batter into the skillet, tilting to coat evenly, and cook until golden on the underside. Turn over with a spatula, or flip. Cook the second side, then slide out of the skillet onto a plate.

3. Repeat with the remaining batter until you have made eight thin pancakes and all the batter is used.

4. Put all the ingredients for the filling into a bowl and beat together until smooth. Divide among the pancakes, spreading into a thick circle over the center. Brush the edges with the reserved egg white. Fold in the sides, then fold the top edge down and the bottom edge up so that the filling is completely covered and you have a square parcel. Put join side downward on a baking sheet, cover with plastic wrap, and chill overnight, if liked.

5. Put all the ingredients for the compote into a small saucepan and warm through.

6. Heat the butter in a large skillet and reheat the pancakes (in batches if necessary) with the seam uppermost, then turn over carefully and cook until piping hot. Arrange two blintz on each serving plate, spoon the warm compote around, then dust with a little sifted confectioners' sugar.

CHOCOLATE CHERRY CREPES

These wonderfully thin, French-style pancakes use frozen cherries. If you would rather use bottled cherries, then add some of the juice in place of the measured water to cook them in.

SERVES 4

¾ cup all-purpose flour
2 tablespoons unsweatened cocoa
1 egg plus 1 egg yolk
1 tablespoon sunflower oil, plus
   extra for frying
1 cup milk
Sifted confectioners' sugar,
   for dusting

FILLING

2½ cups frozen pitted red cherries
2 teaspoons cornstarch
¼ cup superfine sugar
1 scant cup mascarpone cheese
⅔ cup custard or vanilla pudding
1 teaspoon vanilla extract

1. Sift the flour and cocoa into a bowl. Add the egg, egg yolk, and oil, then gradually beat in the milk until smooth. Let stand for 15 minutes.

2. For the filling, put the cherries into a saucepan. Mix the cornstarch to a smooth paste with a little of the water, then add to the pan with the remaining water and the sugar. Cook over medium heat for 4–5 minutes, stirring, until the sauce has thickened and the cherries are slightly softened.

3. Lightly beat the mascarpone cheese, custard, and vanilla extract together in a bowl until smooth.

4. Heat a little oil in a small skillet, then pour the excess into a cup. Add 2–3 spoonfuls of the crepe batter to the skillet, tilting to swirl into a thin lacy pancake. Cook for 1–2 minutes until browned, then turn over with a spatula and cook the second side. Slide the pancake onto a plate and repeat with the remaining batter to make eight crepes.

5. Divide the crepes among serving plates. Spoon the mascarpone mixture over the center of each pancake, top with the cherry filling, then fold each pancake into quarters. Dust lightly with sifted confectioners' sugar and serve immediately.

BAKLAVA PANCAKE STACK

SERVES 4

¾ cup all-purpose flour
1 egg plus 1 egg yolk
1 cup milk
Sunflower oil for frying
Whole-milk yogurt, to serve
SYRUP
½ cup walnut pieces
½ lemon
½ orange
Scant ½ cup superfine sugar
Pinch of grated nutmeg
½ teaspoon ground cinnamon
½ teaspoon rose water

1. Preheat the broiler. Sift the flour into a bowl. Add the egg and egg yolk, then gradually beat in the milk until smooth. Let stand for 15 minutes.

2. Meanwhile, make the syrup. Lightly toast the walnuts on a piece of aluminum foil under the preheated broiler. Pare the rind off the lemon and orange with a swivel-bladed vegetable peeler and cut into thin strips. Squeeze the juice and add to a saucepan with the rinds, 1 cup of water, the sugar, and spices.

3. Simmer over a low heat for 5 minutes, stirring once or twice, until the sugar has dissolved and the liquid has become syrupy. Add the toasted walnuts to the syrup with the rose water. Cook for 2–3 minutes, then remove from the heat.

4. Beat the pancake batter once again. Heat a little oil in a 9-inch skillet, then pour the excess into a cup. Pour just enough batter into the skillet to cover the bottom thinly. Cook until the underside is golden, then turn over with a spatula and cook the second side.

5. Repeat until all the batter has been used and you have at least four pancakes. Reheat the syrup to boiling.

6. Put one of the pancakes on a rimmed plate, spoon over some of the syrup and nuts, then cover with another pancake. Repeat the layers, ending with syrup. Let stand for 10 minutes. Cut into wedges, transfer to serving plates, and serve with spoonfuls of yogurt.

POTATO LATKES

Jewish in origin, these grated potato and onion pancakes look a little like the Swiss rosti. Here, they are topped with horseradish and scallion-flavored yogurt and caraway-spiked diced beets.

SERVES 4

4 small baking potatoes, about 1 lb
1 small onion, finely chopped
½ cup all-purpose flour
1 egg, beaten
3 tablespoons sunflower oil
TOPPING
1 cup plain yogurt
1 teaspoon hot horseradish sauce
4 scallions, finely chopped
3 cooked peeled beets, about
   6 oz, diced
1 teaspoon caraway seeds
Salt and ground black pepper

1. Peel and coarsely grate the potatoes, then put into a fine-mesh strainer and press out any water. Transfer to a mixing bowl and add the chopped onion and flour and mix together. Stir in the egg and season with salt and black pepper.

2. Heat 1 tablespoon of the oil in a large skillet and drop large spoonfuls of the mixture into the skillet, spacing them well apart, then flatten slightly. Cook on each side for 2–3 minutes, until golden and the potatoes are cooked through. Lift out of the skillet with a spatula and put onto a heatproof plate. Keep hot in the oven.

3. Continue oiling the skillet and frying the latkes until you have eight pancakes and the mixture is used.

4. While the latkes are frying, spoon the yogurt into a bowl. Add the horseradish, half of the scallions, and a little salt and black pepper and mix. Mix the beets and caraway seeds in a second bowl.

5. Serve two latkes per portion, topped with spoonfuls of the horseradish topping and beets and sprinkled with the remaining scallions.

SEAFOOD PANCAKE PIE

SERVES 4

PANCAKES
¾ cup all-purpose flour
1 egg plus 1 egg yolk
1 cup milk
Sunflower oil for frying
Salad or green spring vegetables,
   to serve

FILLING
10 oz salmon or trout fillet in one
   piece
14-oz bag frozen seafood selection
   (to include shrimp, mussels, and
   squid), defrosted
4 tablespoons butter
Scant ½ cup all-purpose flour
1 bay leaf
2½ cups milk
½ cup freshly grated Parmesan
   cheese
Salt and ground black pepper

1. Sift the flour into a bowl, add a little salt and black pepper, the whole egg, and the egg yolk, then gradually beat in the milk until smooth. Let stand for 15 minutes.

2. Preheat the oven to 375°F. Put the salmon into a steaming basket set over a pan of boiling water. Cover and cook for 12 minutes or until the flesh is pale pink all the way through and breaks into flakes when pressed with a knife in the center of the fillet. Turn the mixed seafood into a fine-mesh strainer, rinse with cold water, and drain again, then set aside.

3. Heat the butter in a medium saucepan, stir in the flour, and add the bay leaf. Gradually beat in the milk and bring to a boil, beating until smooth and thickened. Season lightly, then stir in half the cheese.

4. Heat a little oil in a medium skillet with the same diameter as a round 5-cup, 2-inch deep ovenproof dish. Pour the excess oil into a cup then pour in just enough batter to thinly coat the bottom of the skillet. Cook until the underside is golden, then turn over with a spatula and cook the second side. Slide out onto a plate then repeat, oiling the skillet as needed, until all the batter is used and you have four or five pancakes.

5. Put one of the pancakes in the bottom of the dish and pour over a little of the sauce, discarding the bay leaf. Top with some of the salmon and the seafood. Cover with a second pancake then repeat the layers, finishing with the sauce. Sprinkle with the remaining cheese.

6. Bake in the preheated oven for 35 minutes until golden.

7. Cut into wedges and serve with salad or green spring vegetables.

HEMP & SUNFLOWER SEED CREPES

Hemp is a surprisingly good source of protein and essential fatty acids. Either buy as flour from good health food stores or buy the seeds and grind them into flour in a spice mill or blender.

SERVES 4

½ cup hemp flour
½ cup all-purpose flour
1 egg plus 1 egg yolk
1 tablespoon sunflower oil, plus
　　extra for frying
1¼ cups milk
¼ cup sunflower seeds
TO SERVE
Superfine sugar
2 lemons, cut into wedges

1. Put the flours into a bowl and add the whole egg, egg yolk, and oil. Gradually beat in the milk to make a smooth batter. Let stand for 15 minutes, then beat the batter once again.

2. Heat a little oil in a 7-inch skillet, then pour the excess into a cup. Pour 2–3 tablespoons of the batter into the skillet, tilting it to coat evenly, then sprinkle with a few of the sunflower seeds. Cook until browned on the underside, then turn over with a spatula, or flip, and cook the second side. Slide out of the skillet onto a plate and keep hot.

3. Repeat with the remaining batter, oiling the skillet as needed, until you have made eight thin pancakes and all the batter has been used.

4. Fold the pancakes and divide among serving plates. Sprinkle with sugar and serve immediately with lemon wedges to squeeze over.

BLACKBERRY & APPLE PANCAKES

These were traditionally made by British fruit pickers a hundred years ago or more and baked in saucers. Nowadays, they are easier to bake in individual metal tart pans, avoiding the hazard of the saucers cracking during cooking. The batter rises around the edges slightly and is very similar to the French clafoutis.

SERVES 4

¾ cup all-purpose flour
¼ cup superfine sugar
2 eggs
1¼ cups milk and water mixed
1 tablespoon sunflower oil
2 tablespoons butter
2 apples, cored and sliced,
    but not peeled
Juice of ½ lemon
⅔ cup blackberries, defrosted
    if frozen
Sifted confectioners' sugar,
    for dusting
Whipped cream or sour cream,
    to serve

1. Preheat the oven to 400°F. Sift the flour into a bowl.

2. Add 2 tablespoons of the sugar and the eggs and gradually beat in the milk and water mixture until smooth. Let stand for 30 minutes.

3. Divide the oil and butter among four 5-inch metal tart pans (do not use removable-bottom pans). Toss the apple slices with the lemon, then add to the pans with the blackberries. Sprinkle with the remaining 2 tablespoons of the sugar.

4. Stand the pans on a baking sheet and cook in the preheated oven for 5 minutes, until the pans are sizzling hot.

5. Beat the batter again briefly, then pour into the hot pans. Cook for 20 minutes, until golden brown.

6. Dust with confectioners' sugar and quickly transfer the puddings still in their pans to serving plates. Top each with a spoonful of whipped cream or sour cream. Serve immediately because they quickly lose volume.

BUTTERMILK PANCAKES

Light and fluffy and so easy to make, these buttermilk pancakes are bound to become a firm family favorite.

SERVES 4

½ tablespoon butter
1⅓ cups self-rising flour
1 teaspoon baking soda
3 tablespoons granulated sugar
1 egg
¾ cup buttermilk
TO SERVE
Butter
Maple syrup

1. Melt the butter in a small pan. Sift the flour and baking soda together into a bowl and stir in the sugar. Beat the egg and buttermilk together and gradually beat into the dry ingredients with the melted butter to make a smooth paste.

2. Heat a nonstick skillet until hot and drop in large spoonfuls of the batter. Cook for 3 minutes, or until bubbles appear on the surface. Flip the pancakes over and cook for another minute. Remove from the skillet to a plate and keep hot. Repeat until all the batter is used.

3. Serve the pancakes as a high stack topped with butter and a generous drizzle of maple syrup.

WAFFLES

ROQUEFORT WAFFLES WITH PROSCIUTTO

Give a basic waffle the five-star treatment with this gourmet mix of ingredients. Look out for chilled sun-blush tomatoes with their delicate taste and wonderful exotic color on the deli aisle in the supermarket. If you can't find them, substitute sun-dried tomatoes in oil sold in jars.

SERVES 4

1 cup all-purpose flour
1 teaspoon baking powder
¼ teaspoon baking soda
5 oz Roquefort cheese, rind
  removed, diced
1 egg
⅔ cup milk
5 oz chilled sunblush tomatoes
  in olive oil
4 slices of prosciutto
1½ cups arugula leaves
Salt and ground black pepper

1. Preheat the waffle machine. Sift the flour, baking powder, and baking soda into a mixing bowl. Add a little salt and black pepper and one-third of the cheese. Beat the egg and milk together, then beat into the dry ingredients until smooth.

2. Pour the batter into the waffle machine, close the lid, and cook until browned and well risen.

3. Quickly pour 1 tablespoon of oil from the tomatoes into a skillet, add the prosciutto, and cook for 2–3 minutes, until crisp.

4. Transfer the waffles to serving plates. Toss the arugula with a little oil from the tomatoes, then arrange on the waffles with the drained tomatoes and remaining cheese. Cut the prosciutto into strips and arrange on top of the waffles. Serve immediately.

BRIE & CRANBERRY WAFFLES

Incredibly quick and easy to put together, this smart-looking brunch will impress your guests. Vary the type of cheese according to your favorite— Camembert and dolcelatte both work well.

SERVES 4

1 cup all-purpose flour
1 teaspoon baking powder
¼ teaspoon baking soda
2 tablespoons butter, melted
1 egg
⅔ cup milk
3 tablespoons olive oil
2 teaspoons balsamic vinegar
1 generous cup spinach, arugula, and watercress salad
6 oz Brie cheese, thinly sliced
3 tablespoons cranberry sauce
Salt and ground black pepper

1. Preheat the waffle machine. Sift the flour, baking powder, and baking soda into a mixing bowl. Season with a little salt and black pepper. Mix the butter, egg, and milk together in a separate bowl, then gradually beat into the dry ingredients until smooth.

2. Pour the batter into the waffle machine, close the lid, and cook until browned and well risen.

3. Meanwhile, mix the oil, vinegar, and a little salt and black pepper in a salad bowl. Add the salad greens and toss together.

4. Transfer the waffles to serving plates, top with the salad, then the slices of Brie and spoonfuls of cranberry sauce. Serve immediately.

BEERY WAFFLES WITH HAM & CHEESE

For all beer fans, this is the perfect partnership. Either open a new bottle—if you plan on serving beer at brunch—or use up a little leftover flat beer from the night before. It adds a surprisingly strong flavor.

SERVES 4

1 cup all-purpose flour
1 teaspoon baking powder
¼ teaspoon baking soda
1 egg
⅔ cup blonde beer
4 tablespoons butter, at room
    temperature
2 teaspoons whole-grain mustard
6 thin slices of honey roast ham
1 cup shredded cheddar cheese
Salt and ground black pepper
WAFFLES
Sliced dill pickles
Watercress leaves

1. Preheat the waffle machine and preheat the broiler.

2. Sift the flour, baking powder, and baking soda into a bowl and season with a little salt and black pepper. Add the egg, then gradually beat in the beer until smooth.

3. Spoon the batter into the waffle machine, close the lid, and cook until browned and well risen.

4. Meanwhile, put the butter in a bowl and beat in the mustard.

5. Transfer the waffles to the broiler pan and dot with the mustard butter. Tear the ham into wide strips and fold attractively on top of the waffles. Sprinkle with the cheese and broil until the cheese is bubbling, keeping a watchful eye that the waffles don't overcook around the edges.

6. Arrange the waffles on serving plates, tuck the sliced pickles into the folds of ham, and sprinkle with a little watercress. Serve immediately.

CHOCOLATE BANANA WAFFLES

Popular with all ages, this flavor combination doesn't need to be reserved just for brunch. The sauce can be made the night before and stored in the refrigerator. Warm any leftovers to spoon over ice cream.

SERVES 4

CHOCOLATE SAUCE

5 oz dark chocolate, broken into
   pieces
⅔ cup milk
¼ cup superfine sugar

CHANTILLY CREAM

1 cup heavy cream
2 tablespoons confectioners' sugar
1 teaspoon vanilla extract

WAFFLES

3 bananas
Juice of 1 lemon
1 cup all-purpose flour
1 teaspoon baking powder
¼ teaspoon baking soda
2 tablespoons butter, melted
1 egg
⅔ cup milk

1. First, make the sauce by gently heating the chocolate, milk, and sugar together in a small saucepan. Stir until the sauce is smooth, then set aside.

2. Pour the cream into a bowl and add the sugar and vanilla extract. Beat until it forms soft swirls, then set aside.

3. Mash one of the bananas on a plate with a little of the lemon juice, then slice the remaining two bananas and toss with the rest of the lemon juice.

4. Preheat the waffle machine. For the waffles, sift the flour, baking powder, and baking soda into a mixing bowl. Beat the butter, egg, and milk together in a separate bowl, then gradually beat into the dry ingredients until smooth. Beat in the mashed banana.

5. Spoon the batter into the waffle machine, close the lid, and cook until browned and well risen. Transfer the waffles to serving plates.

6. Top with spoonfuls of Chantilly cream, sliced bananas, and a drizzle of chocolate sauce. Pour the remaining sauce into a small pitcher and hand around to diners.

SPICED WAFFLES WITH SHERRY RAISINS

An unusual flavor combination, but one that really works well together. Warming the raisins and soaking in sherry beforehand certainly gives them a lift. If you have some Madeira, Pineau des Charentes, or Pedro Ximenez, you may also like to use one of them as a delicious alternative.

SERVES 4

½ cup raisins
¼ cup sherry
1 cup all-purpose flour
1 teaspoon ground cinnamon
1 teaspoon baking powder
¼ teaspoon baking soda
2 tablespoons butter, melted
1 egg
⅔ cup milk
1 cup ricotta cheese
3 tablespoons pine nuts, lightly
   toasted
Maple syrup, to serve

1. Put the raisins and sherry in a small bowl and warm in the microwave on full power for 30 seconds. Set aside for 30 minutes.

2. Preheat the waffle machine. Sift the flour, cinnamon, baking powder, and baking soda into a mixing bowl. Mix the butter, egg, and milk together in a separate bowl, then beat into the dry ingredients.

3. Spoon the batter into the waffle machine, close the lid, and cook until browned and well risen.

4. Arrange the waffles on serving plates and top with spoonfuls of ricotta, some soaked raisins, and a sprinkling of pine nuts. Drizzle with maple syrup and serve immediately.

CHOCOLATE MINT WAFFLES

These dark chocolate waffles, topped with whipped cream flavored with green speckles of fresh garden mint and finished with fresh raspberries or tiny summer strawberries, capture the very essence of summer.

SERVES 4

Generous ¾ cup all-purpose flour
3 tablespoons unsweetened cocoa
1 teaspoon baking powder
¼ teaspoon baking soda
2 tablespoons superfine sugar
2 tablespoons butter, melted
1 egg
⅔ cup milk

TO FINISH

1 cup heavy cream
3 tablespoons superfine sugar
3 tablespoons chopped mint, plus
   extra to decorate
Fresh strawberries and raspberries
Sifted confectioners' sugar, for
   dusting

1. Preheat the waffle machine. Sift the flour, cocoa, baking powder, and baking soda into a mixing bowl, then add the sugar. Mix the butter, egg, and milk together in a separate bowl, then gradually beat into the dry ingredients until smooth.

2. Pour the batter into the waffle machine, close the lid, and cook until browned and well risen.

3. Meanwhile, pour the cream into a separate bowl, add the sugar and mint, and whip until the cream forms soft swirls.

4. Transfer the waffles to serving plates. Top with spoonfuls of the cream and a sprinkling of fruit and tiny mint leaves. Dust lightly with sifted confectioners' sugar and serve immediately.

HAZELNUT WAFFLES WITH MAPLE SYRUP

Don't be tempted to skip toasting the nuts because it really brings out their flavor. You can always toast a larger amount, use half now, and then store the extras, when cold, in a sealed storage jar for another time.

SERVES 4

⅓ cup hazelnuts
1 cup all-purpose flour
1 teaspoon baking powder
¼ teaspoon baking soda
2 tablespoons butter, melted
1 egg
⅔ cup milk

TOPPING
3 oz dark chocolate, roughly chopped
A few toasted hazelnuts, roughly
  chopped

TO SERVE
Maple syrup
Heavy cream

1. Preheat the broiler. Put the hazelnuts on a piece of aluminum foil on the broiler rack and toast under the preheated broiler until golden. Carefully transfer to a cutting board and finely chop.

2. Preheat the waffle machine. Sift the flour, baking powder, and baking soda into a mixing bowl and stir in the chopped nuts. Mix the butter, egg, and milk together in a separate bowl, then gradually beat into the dry ingredients to make a smooth batter.

3. Spoon the batter into the waffle machine, close the lid, and cook until browned and well risen.

4. Arrange the waffles on serving plates, cutting in half diagonally, if desired. Sprinkle with the chocolate and hazelnuts, and drizzle with maple syrup and cream to serve.

WAFFLES WITH HONEYED FIGS

Although figs are available in the winter months, this recipe is best made in the summer, when Californian figs are at their best and lavender can be picked from the yard.

SERVES 4

8 figs
3 tablespoons butter
4 teaspoons lavender honey
2–3 fresh or dried lavender flowers (optional), plus extra to decorate
Whole-milk yogurt, to serve

WAFFLES

1 cup whole-wheat flour
1 teaspoon baking powder
¼ teaspoon baking soda
2 teaspoons superfine sugar
2 tablespoons butter, melted
1 egg
¾ cup milk

1. Preheat the oven to 375°F and line a baking pan with aluminum foil.

2. Make a cross cut halfway down into each fig and place them into the prepared baking pan. Cut the butter into eight and put a cube into the center of each fig. Add a little honey and a few lavender petals, if using.

3. Bake the figs in the preheated oven for 5–10 minutes, depending on their ripeness, until hot and tender.

4. Preheat the waffle machine. Mix the flour, baking powder, and baking soda together in a mixing bowl. Beat the butter, egg, and milk together in a separate bowl, then gradually beat into the dry ingredients until smooth.

5. Spoon the batter into the waffle machine, close the lid, and cook until browned and well risen.

6. Divide the waffles among serving plates and top with the baked figs and their buttery juices. Decorate with extra lavender flowers, if desired, and serve immediately with spoonfuls of yogurt.

THYME WAFFLES WITH SAUTÉED MUSHROOMS

Nothing beats the flavor of fresh herbs. Even if you don't have a growing
space, keep a pot of fresh thyme on your windowsill and tear off a few leaves
as you need them.

SERVES 4

1 cup all-purpose flour
1 teaspoon baking powder
¼ teaspoon baking soda
1 tablespoon fresh thyme leaves,
  plus extra to garnish
1 egg
2 tablespoons olive oil
⅔ cup milk

TOPPING
2 tablespoons olive oil
2 tablespoons butter
1 garlic clove, finely chopped
5 oz exotic mushrooms, large ones
  sliced
3¼ cups thickly sliced white
  mushrooms, about 8 oz
2 tablespoons cider vinegar
⅓ cup heavy cream
Salt and ground black pepper

1. Sift the flour, baking powder, and baking soda into a mixing bowl, then
stir in the thyme and season with salt and black pepper. Mix the egg, oil,
and milk together in a separate bowl and set aside.

2. To make the topping, heat the oil and butter over a high heat in a
skillet, add the garlic and mushrooms, and fry for 2–3 minutes, stirring,
until the mushrooms are golden.

3. Add the vinegar, cook for 1 minute, then reduce the heat slightly. Add
the cream and a little salt and black pepper. Cook for 2 minutes more.

4. Preheat the waffle machine. Beat the egg mixture into the dry
ingredients until smooth. Spoon the batter into the waffle machine, close
the lid, and cook until browned and well risen.

5. Arrange the waffles on serving plates. Reheat the mushrooms, if
necessary, then spoon over the waffles. Garnish with a few extra thyme
leaves and a little black pepper.

ORANGE WAFFLES WITH CLEMENTINES

SERVES 4

4 clementines, peeled and left whole
4 tablespoons butter
2 tablespoons confectioners' sugar
¼ cup pistachios, roughly chopped
1 tablespoon Grand Marnier
WAFFLES
1 cup all-purpose flour
1 teaspoon baking powder
¼ teaspoon baking soda
Grated zest of 1 clementine or
  ½ orange
1 tablespoon confectioners' sugar,
  plus extra for dusting
2 tablespoons butter, melted
1 egg
⅔ cup milk
2 tablespoons Grand Marnier
Plain yogurt, to serve

1. Preheat the oven to 350°F. Cut four pieces of aluminum foil or non-stick parchment paper large enough to wrap each clementine and put one clementine on each piece. Mix the butter with the confectioners' sugar, pistachios, and liqueur. Spoon the flavored butter over the top of each clementine, then enclose in the foil or paper, twisting the edges to secure. Place on a baking sheet and cook in the preheated oven for 10 minutes, until hot.

2. Preheat the waffle machine. Sift the flour, baking powder, and baking soda into a mixing bowl then add the fruit zest and sugar. Mix the butter, egg, milk, and liqueur together in a separate bowl, then gradually beat into the dry ingredients until smooth.

3. Spoon the batter into the waffle machine, close the lid, and cook until browned and well risen.

4. Cut the waffles in half and transfer to serving plates. Unwrap the clementines and put one of top of each waffle. Add a spoonful of plain yogurt, then drizzle with the buttery juices. Dust with a little sifted confectioners' sugar and serve immediately.

SPINACH WAFFLES WITH SHRIMP

SERVES 4

2 cups baby leaf spinach
1 tablespoon olive oil
6 scallions, chopped
2 cups cherry tomatoes, about 10 oz, halved
4 oz large frozen shrimp, defrosted
Small bunch of basil
Juice of ½ lemon
1 cup all-purpose flour
1 teaspoon baking powder
¼ teaspoon baking soda
Pinch of grated nutmeg
1 egg
⅔ cup milk
⅓ cup mascarpone cheese
Salt and ground black pepper

1. Rinse the spinach with cold water, then drain roughly so that a little water still clings to the leaves. Heat a skillet, then add the spinach and cook (without oil) for 2 minutes, stirring, until just wilted. Scoop onto a cutting board.

2. Heat the oil in the skillet and add the scallions and tomatoes. Fry for 2 minutes, until softened. Add the shrimp and half the basil, torn into pieces, and season with a little salt and black pepper. Fry for 2–3 minutes, stirring, until the shrimp are piping hot, then stir through the lemon juice.

3. Preheat the waffle machine. Sift the flour, baking powder, baking soda, and a pinch of grated nutmeg into a bowl. Season with salt and black pepper. Finely chop the spinach and add it to the bowl, then add the egg. Gradually beat in the milk until the batter is smooth.

4. Spoon the batter into the waffle machine, close the lid, and cook until the waffles are golden and well risen. Lift out of the machine, cut in half, and arrange the halves on serving plates. Top with spoonfuls of mascarpone cheese, the hot shrimp mixture, and the remaining basil leaves.

PUMPKIN WAFFLES WITH CHILI SAUCE

Here is a healthy option for all those who are trying to reduce their fat intake. If you are feeling extra hungry, you might like to add a few peeled shrimp to the cottage cheese—just make sure to defrost them thoroughly if frozen.

SERVES 4

1 tablespoon butter
1 cup coarsely grated pumpkin or butternut squash, about 4 oz
1 cup all-purpose flour
1 teaspoon baking powder
¼ teaspoon baking soda
½ teaspoon cumin seeds, roughly crushed
1 egg
¼ cup milk
Salt and ground black pepper

TO SERVE

1 cup cottage or ricotta cheese
⅓ cup Thai sweet chili dipping sauce
2 scallions, chopped
Small bunch of cilantro

1. Heat the butter in a skillet, over medium heat, add the pumpkin or squash and fry for 2 minutes, stirring, until softened.

2. Preheat the waffle machine. Sift the flour, baking powder, and baking soda into a mixing bowl, then add the cumin seeds and season with salt and black pepper. Add the pumpkin, egg, and milk and mix together to make a stiff batter.

3. Spoon the batter into the waffle machine, close the lid, and cook until browned and well risen.

4. Arrange the waffles on serving plates, cutting in half diagonally, if desired. Top with spoonfuls of cheese, a drizzle of chili sauce, and a sprinkling of chopped scallions and torn cilantro leaves.

CARIBBEAN COCONUT WAFFLES

Canned coconut milk is used instead of dairy milk, giving these waffles a light delicate flavor. For a special brunch, create a little drama by adding 3 tablespoons of rum to the warm pineapple. Heat until the rum just begins to bubble, then flame with a taper and spoon over the waffles as soon as the flames have subsided.

SERVES 4

1 cup all-purpose flour
1 teaspoon baking powder
¼ teaspoon baking soda
1 tablespoon superfine sugar
1 egg
¾ cup coconut milk
Whole-milk yogurt, to serve

TOPPING

½ large pineapple, peeled
2 tablespoons butter
Grated zest and juice of 1 lime
2 tablespoons superfine sugar
Seeds from ½ pomegranate

1. Sift the flour, baking powder, and baking soda into a bowl. Add the sugar and mix together, then set aside.

2. To make the topping, slice the pineapple, cut away the core, then dice the flesh. Heat the butter in a skillet, add the pineapple, and fry for 3–4 minutes, stirring, until hot but not browned. Stir in the lime zest and juice and the sugar and sprinkle with the pomegranate seeds. Cook for 1–2 minutes, then remove from the heat.

3. Preheat the waffle machine. Add the egg to the dry ingredients, then gradually beat in the coconut milk until smooth.

4. Spoon the batter into the waffle machine, close the lid, and cook until browned and well risen.

5. Cut the waffles in half diagonally, then transfer the waffles to serving plates. Top with spoonfuls of yogurt and the warm pineapple mix.

PEACH MELBA WAFFLES

All the classic ingredients for a peach melba sundae but served on a hot waffle with a spoonful of yogurt.

SERVES 4

TOPPING
2 cups raspberries, plus extra to garnish
2 tablespoons confectioners' sugar
Juice of ½ lemon

WAFFLES
1 cup all-purpose flour
1 teaspoon baking powder
¼ teaspoon baking soda
2 teaspoons confectioners' sugar
2 tablespoons butter, melted
1 egg
⅔ cup milk

TO SERVE
¾ cup plain yogurt
2 peaches, halved, pitted, and sliced

1. First, make the melba sauce by pureeing the raspberries in a blender or food processor, then pressing them through a fine-mesh strainer to remove the seeds. Stir the sugar and lemon juice into the puree then pour into a pitcher.

2. Preheat the waffle machine. Sift the flour, baking powder, baking soda, and confectioners' sugar into a bowl. Mix the butter, egg, and milk together in a separate bowl, then gradually beat into the dry ingredients until smooth.

3. Spoon the batter into the waffle machine, close the lid, and cook until browned and well risen.

4. Transfer the waffles to serving plates. Top with spoonfuls of yogurt, the peach slices, and raspberries, then drizzle with a little sauce. Serve the waffles immediately.

WAFFLES WITH MIXED BERRIES

SERVES 4

6 tablespoons butter
2 eggs
½ cup milk
1 cup whole-wheat flour
1 teaspoon baking powder
¼ teaspoon baking soda
3 tablespoons confectioners' sugar,
   plus extra for dusting
Grated zest and juice of ½ lemon
3 cups frozen mixed berries,
   defrosted
1 mint sprig, plus extra to decorate
Sour cream, to serve

1. Melt the butter, then let it to cool a little.

2. Separate the eggs. Add the egg yolks to the milk and beat together lightly. Add 1 tablespoonful of the melted butter to the milk mixture and work in lightly with a fork.

3. Preheat the waffle machine. Sift the flour, baking powder, and baking soda into a mixing bowl. Make a well in the flour and gradually beat in the milk and the remaining butter. Beat the egg whites until stiff enough to hold firm peaks, then fold into the batter with 2 tablespoons of the confectioners' sugar and the lemon zest.

4. Spoon the batter into the waffle machine, close the lid, and cook until browned and well risen.

5. Put the lemon juice and fruit into a saucepan with the mint and heat gently until the juices run, stirring to prevent the fruit from sticking.

6. Transfer the waffles to serving plates. Top each waffle with some of the fruit. Dust with a little confectioners' sugar and add a mint sprig to decorate. Serve with sour cream.

LEMON WAFFLES WITH MARMALADE SAUCE

Chances are you will have all the ingredients for these tangy waffles in the pantry and fruit bowl. If you don't have any whiskey, or would rather not use it, then add extra orange juice instead, either freshly squeezed or from a carton—both will work just as well.

SERVES 4

1 cup all-purpose flour
1 teaspoon baking powder
¼ teaspoon baking soda
2 teaspoons superfine sugar
Grated zest of 1 lemon
2 tablespoons sunflower oil
1 egg
⅔ cup milk
Plain yogurt or whipped cream,
   to serve

WHISKEY MARMALADE SAUCE
1 teaspoon cornstarch
Juice of ½ lemon
¼ cup orange marmalade
3 tablespoons orange juice
3 tablespoons whiskey

1. Sift the flour, baking powder, and baking soda into a bowl, then stir in the sugar and lemon zest. Mix the oil, egg, and milk in a separate bowl, then set aside.

2. To make the sauce, mix the cornstarch and lemon juice together in a small saucepan, then add the remaining ingredients. Bring to a boil, stirring, and cook for 2–3 minutes until thickened.

3. Preheat the waffle machine. Beat the egg mixture into the dry ingredients until smooth. Spoon the batter into the machine, close the lid, and cook until browned and well risen.

4. Transfer the waffles to serving plates. Top with spoonfuls of yogurt or whipped cream, and drizzle the sauce over. Serve immediately.

CAPPUCCINO WAFFLES

All the flavors of a cappuccino in a waffle, with the added luxury of a dash of coffee cream liqueur added to the whipped cream topping. If you are feeling really decadent, then drizzle with a little warm chocolate sauce (see page 104).

SERVES 4

3 teaspoons instant coffee
2 teaspoons boiling water
1 cup all-purpose flour
1 teaspoon baking powder
¼ teaspoon baking soda
1 tablespoon superfine sugar
2 tablespoons sunflower oil
1 egg
⅔ cup milk
1 cup heavy cream
2 tablespoons confectioners' sugar
3 tablespoons coffee cream liqueur
   (optional)

TO DECORATE
Chocolate curls
Sifted chocolate drink powder,
   for dusting

1. Dissolve the coffee in the boiling water, then let cool.

2. Preheat the waffle machine. Sift the flour, baking powder, and baking soda into a mixing bowl then add the sugar. Beat the dissolved coffee with the oil, egg, and milk in a separate bowl, then gradually mix into the dry ingredients until smooth.

3. Spoon the batter into the waffle machine, close the lid, and cook until browned and well risen.

4. Meanwhile, whip the cream with the confectioners' sugar until soft swirls form. Gradually beat in the cream liqueur, if using.

5. Transfer the waffles to serving plates. Top with spoonfuls of the cream, chocolate curls, and a dusting of sifted chocolate powder. Serve immediately.

TIP
To make chocolate curls, run a swivel-bladed vegetable peeler over the underside of a block of chocolate. If the curls are too small, warm the chocolate in the microwave on full power for 10 seconds, then try again.

TOAST
TOPPERS

EGGS BENEDICT

SERVES 4

HOLLANDAISE SAUCE
2 tablespoons white wine vinegar
14 tablespoons (1¾ sticks) unsalted
    butter
2 egg yolks
Dash of lemon juice, if needed
TO FINISH
8 slices of Canadian-style bacon
4 English muffins, halved
Butter for spreading
1 teaspoon whole-grain mustard
4 eggs
Salt and ground black pepper
Watercress, to garnish

1. To make the sauce, put the vinegar and a little salt and black pepper into a small saucepan and boil for 2–3 minutes, until reduced by half. Pour into a cup and let cool. Wash and dry the pan, then gently melt the butter in it. Pour the clear butter into a jug, leaving behind the white milk solids.

2. Broil the bacon until golden. Toast the muffins, only on the cut side, then spread with a little butter and the mustard. Top four halves with the bacon and keep hot.

3. Put the cooled vinegar, egg yolks, and 1 tablespoon water into a large bowl set over a saucepan of simmering water, checking that the bottom of the bowl is not touching the water. Beat for 2 minutes, until thick and frothy, then gradually beat in the warm (not hot) clear butter, a few drops at a time, beating until smooth before adding more. Continue until all the butter has been added and the sauce is thick. Don't try to hurry this process or the sauce will "split."

4. Remove the bowl from the heat, and make sure that the water in the pan below is gently simmering. Break an egg into a cup, then slide the egg into the water. Repeat with the remaining eggs. Poach for 3–4 minutes, until the whites are set and the yolks done as you prefer.

5. Carefully lift out the eggs with a slotted spoon and drain well. Place on the bacon-topped muffins and transfer to serving plates. Add the remaining muffin halves.

6. Thin the sauce with a few drops of lemon juice and season, if necessary. Spoon over the eggs, garnish with watercress and coarsely ground black pepper, and serve immediately.

TALEGGIO & WILD MUSHROOMS

This is mouth-watering dish delicious with the smoky flavors of wild mushroom and the gentle saltiness of the Taleggio cheese.

SERVES 2

2 tablespoons butter
2 tablespoons olive oil
4 oz mixed wild mushrooms, trimmed
1 small garlic clove, chopped
2 tablespoons chopped parsley
2 large, all-butter croissants
4 oz Taleggio cheese, sliced
Salt and ground black pepper

1. Melt the butter with the olive oil in a skillet over medium heat. Add the mushrooms, garlic, and parsley and fry until soft and golden. Season well with salt and black pepper, remove from the heat, and let cool.

2. Split the croissants in half horizontally. Top the bases with the Taleggio slices and the mushrooms, then place the remaining halves of the croissants on top.

3. Set a sandwich grill to "melt." Place the croissants on the bottom plate and lower the top so that it rests gently on the croissants. This will toast the croissants and gently melt the cheese filling. Remove from the sandwich grill and serve immediately.

PIGS IN BLANKETS

If you have young children who are eager to help cook, then this is the ideal recipe for them.

TIP
Ketchup fans might like to squirt a thin line straight from the bottle, diagonally down the center of the bread before adding the frankfurters.

MAKES 10

10 slices medium-cut white bread, crusts removed
11½-oz chilled vacuum-packed frankfurters
4 tablespoons butter
1 tablespoon maple syrup
1 teaspoon Dijon mustard

1. Preheat the oven to 375°F.

2. Flatten each slice of bread with a rolling pin and neaten the edges with a knife, if necessary.

3. Lay a frankfurter diagonally across each slice of bread. Roll each bread around each frankfurter and secure the seams with half a toothpick.

4. Warm the butter, syrup, and mustard together in a small saucepan or microwave in a bowl for 30 seconds on full power. Stir together, then brush over the outside of the bread.

5. Place on a baking sheet and cook in the preheated oven for 12–15 minutes, until the bread is golden and crisp. Cool slightly, remove the toothpicks, and serve stacked on a plate.

HERBY SCRAMBLED EGGS WITH GRUYÈRE

Delicious and satisfying as it is, if you want something more substantial serve with crispy bacon slices and broiled tomatoes.

SERVES 2

3 eggs
⅓ cup milk
Dash of Tabasco sauce
2 tablespoons finely chopped chives
2 tablespoons finely chopped chervil
1 teaspoon finely chopped tarragon
2 tablespoons butter
4 thick slices sourdough bread
¾ cup finely shredded sharp Gruyère
  cheese
Salt and ground black pepper
Crispy bacon slices, to serve
  (optional)

1. Lightly beat the eggs in a bowl with the milk, Tabasco sauce, the herbs, and salt and black pepper to taste.

2. Melt the butter in a nonstick pan over medium heat. When the butter is beginning to froth, pour in the egg mixture and stir gently with a fork. Let cook slowly, stirring occasionally, until the eggs are almost cooked. Remove from the heat. Add more salt and black pepper to taste, if necessary.

3. Spoon the scrambled egg mixture onto two slices of sourdough bread and sprinkle with the grated Gruyère.

4. Top with the remaining slices of bread and toast in a sandwich grill for 2–3 minutes, or according to the manufacturer's instructions, until the bread is golden and crisp. Serve immediately with slices of crispy bacon, if using.

GRAVLAX WITH CREAM CHEESE

This is a great alternative to the traditional smoked salmon and cream cheese bagel. Gravlax has a milder flavor, because the salmon is cured with salt, sugar, dill, and black pepper.

SERVES 2

2 poppy and sesame seed bagels, cut in half horizontally
½ cup cream cheese
6 oz gravlax, finely sliced
2 tablespoons chopped chives
Ground black pepper

1. Place the bagels, cut side down, on a sandwich grill. Without closing the lid, toast them for 2–3 minutes, until golden. Remove from the grill.

2. Spread the bases of the bagels with the cream cheese, then top with the gravlax. Sprinkle with the chopped chives and season with black pepper.

3. Top with the lids and return to the sandwich grill. Lower the top plate and toast for 2–3 minutes, or according to the manufacturer's instructions, until golden and crispy. Serve immediately.

PAIN PERDU

French toast goes gourmet with this upmarket version topped with minted yogurt, fresh summer berries, and a drizzle of honey or syrup. If you would rather not buy brioche, then use thickly sliced white bread instead.

SERVES 4

1 cup whole-milk yogurt
2 tablespoons chopped mint
4 thick slices brioche
2 eggs
⅓ cup milk
4 tablespoons butter
2 cups raspberries
1 cup blueberries
⅓ cup honey or light corn syrup
A few extra mint leaves, to decorate
   (optional)
Sifted confectioners' icing, for dusting

1. Mix the yogurt with the mint and spoon into a small bowl. Cut the brioche slices in half diagonally. Beat the eggs and milk together in a shallow dish.

2. Heat half the butter in a skillet. Dip half the bread, a triangle at a time, into the egg mixture until coated on both sides, then add to the skillet. Cook over medium heat until the undersides are golden. Turn over and cook the second side, then take out of the skillet and keep hot on a plate.

3. Melt the remaining butter in the skillet, then dip and cook the remaining pieces of bread.

4. Arrange two triangles per serving on plates, top with spoonfuls of the minted yogurt, the berries, and a drizzle of honey or syrup. Decorate with extra mint leaves, if liked, and dust with sifted confectioners' icing.

CINNAMON MASCARPONE PANINI

The crunch of amaretti cookies contrasts perfectly with the silky smoothness of the sweet cinnamon mascarpone.

SERVES 2

½ cup mascarpone cheese
1 teaspoon ground cinnamon
¼ cup maple syrup
¼ cup Amaretto liqueur
4 slices panettone
½ cup amaretti cookies, crushed

1. Thoroughly mix together the mascarpone, cinnamon, maple syrup, and the liqueur. Spread over two slices of panettone, sprinkle with the crushed cookies, then top with the remaining slices of panettone.

2. Toast in a sandwich grill for 2–3 minutes, or according to the manufacturer's instructions, until the bread is toasted and the filling is beginning to ooze from the sides. Serve immediately.

ORANGE FRENCH TOAST

Made with oranges and raisin bread, this dish is a wonderful, easy-to-make, sweet twist on the traditional French toast.

SERVES 4

2 oranges
6 slices raisin bread
2 eggs
¼ cup milk
¼ teaspoon ground cinnamon
2 tablespoons butter
2 tablespoons sunflower oil

TO SERVE

2 tablespoons sifted confectioners' sugar, for dusting
¼ cup sour cream (optional)

1. Pare the rind from one of the oranges with a zester. Using a small, serrated knife, peel both oranges, then cut between the membranes to separate the segments. Soak the strips of rind in iced water until they curl, then drain on paper towels. Reserve the orange segments.

2. Cut the bread slices in half diagonally. Beat together the eggs, milk, and cinnamon in a shallow dish.

3. Heat half the butter and oil in a large skillet. Quickly dip half the bread triangles in the egg mixture, turning to cover completely, and add to the skillet. Cook in a single layer for 4–5 minutes, turning once, until golden on both sides. Repeat with the remaining butter, oil, and bread.

4. Stack three triangles of bread on each serving plate. Add some orange segments and curls, a spoonful of sour cream, if liked, and dust with confectioners' sugar and serve.

CRUNCHY LEMON CREAM WITH SPONGE TOFFEE

SERVES 2

¼ cup heavy cream, plus extra
   to serve
2 oz sponge toffee, crumbled
1 teaspoon finely grated lemon zest
⅓ cup lemon curd
6 Buttermilk Pancakes (see page 69)
Blueberries, to serve

1. In a small bowl, combine the cream, sponge toffee, lemon zest, and lemon curd.

2. Place a dollop of the lemon cream on a pancake, top with a second pancake and another dollop of lemon cream, then finish with a third pancake. Repeat the process so that you are left with two triple-decker lemon pancakes.

3. Toast the pancake stacks in a sandwich grill for 1–2 minutes, or according to the manufacturer's instructions, until the outside pancakes are toasted and the lemon cream is beginning to ooze from the sides. Serve immediately with some blueberries.

OYSTERS ROCKEFELLER & MELBA TOAST

SERVES 4

3 slices medium-cut white bread
2 tablespoons butter
2 teaspoons chopped chives
2 tablespoons dry white wine
⅓ cup heavy cream
3 teaspoons freshly grated Parmesan
   cheese
12 fresh oysters

1. Preheat the broiler. To make the melba toast, lightly toast the bread on both sides, then trim off the crusts and cut each slice through the center to make six very thin slices, toasted only on one side.

2. Cut each piece into four triangles and put on a baking sheet, toasted side downward. Cook under a medium to low broiler for a few minutes, until the triangles are golden brown and have begun to curl at the points. Put into a basket lined with a napkin.

3. Melt the butter in a small saucepan, add the chives and wine, and boil rapidly for 1 minute. Stir in the cream, cook for 1 minute, then mix in the Parmesan and remove from the heat.

4. To open the oysters, grip an oyster in a dish towel and insert a round-ended or oyster knife between the shells. Slide the knife back and forth until the shells can be separated, then discard the top shells and prop up the lower halves so that the juices are not lost.

5. Carefully holding the oysters in the shells, tilt them over a skillet, and pour the juices into it. Bring to a boil then remove the skillet from the heat and drop in the oysters in a single layer. Return to the heat for 30 seconds, no more or they will be chewy.

6. Reheat the cream mixture, if necessary. Spoon into the oyster shells and place an oyster on top. Serve immediately with the shells arranged on four serving plates and the melba toast to accompany.

HOMEMADE BEANS ON TOAST

Full of cowboy flavor, these rustic beans are best made the day before they are needed, then reheated on the stove top. Serve with toast or, if you are feeling extra hungry, spooned over baked potatoes and topped with broiled bacon or sliced sausages.

SERVES 4

1½ cups dried black-eye peas,
   soaked overnight in cold water
1 onion, chopped
3 tablespoons tomato paste
3 tablespoons light brown sugar
1 tablespoon molasses
2 teaspoons mustard powder
½ teaspoon ground allspice
¼ teaspoon crushed red pepper
   (dried chile flakes)
½ teaspoon salt
2 bay leaves
2 cups water
Ground black pepper
Sprigs of parsley, to garnish
TO SERVE
4 slices toast
Shredded cheddar cheese

1. Drain the soaked beans and put into a medium flameproof casserole. Pour over enough cold water to cover the beans by at least 1 inch, then bring to a boil. Boil rapidly for 10 minutes, skim off any scum, then reduce the heat and simmer for 30–40 minutes, stirring from time to time, until the beans are only just tender.

2. Preheat the oven to 350°F. Drain the beans, then return to the pan and add all the remaining ingredients. Bring to a boil, stirring, then cover the pan and transfer to the preheated oven for 2 hours. Check once or twice during cooking, stir, and fill with a little extra water, if needed.

3. Discard the bay leaves and serve immediately, spooned over toast, sprinkled with a little shredded cheese, and garnished with sprigs of parsley, or let cool and chill overnight in the refrigerator. Reheat when needed on the stove top, adding a little extra water—the beans swell with standing—and stir until piping hot.

SAUSAGE & BACON BURGER

These jumbo burgers should keep the men happy. If they are feeling extra hungry, then add a fried egg, too.

SERVES 4

1 lb good-quality sausages, about
   8 in total
4 oz bacon slices, diced
4 scallions, finely chopped
1 apple, cored and coarsely grated
   (but not peeled)
1 teaspoon mustard powder
1 tablespoon sunflower oil
4 ciabatta rolls or burger buns
3 tomatoes, sliced
Tomato relish or ketchup
Salt and cayenne pepper
Oven-baked potato wedges, to serve
   (optional)

1. Slit the sausages along their length with a small knife and peel away their skins. Put the sausage meat into a mixing bowl and add the bacon, scallions, and apple. Sprinkle in the mustard and season generously with salt and cayenne pepper.

2. Stir the mixture with a spoon until well combined. Divide into four and press each quarter into a burger shape, either in a plastic mold or using floured hands. Chill until required.

3. When ready to serve preheat the broiler. Brush the burgers lightly with the oil and cook under the preheated broiler for 15–18 minutes, turning once or twice, until browned and cooked through. To double check, make a slit through the center of one of the burgers—there should be no hint of pink in the middle.

4. Split the rolls and toast the cut side. Arrange the tomatoes over the lower halves, followed by the burgers and a spoonful of relish or ketchup. Put the remaining halves on top and serve with oven-baked potato wedges, if liked.

SCRAMBLED EGG STACK WITH ANCHOVY TOAST

Forget about plain old scrambled egg on toast—the eggs in this version are served in a large broiled field mushroom on top of anchovy-buttered toast.

SERVES 4

5 tablespoons butter
4 canned anchovy fillets, drained and chopped
4 large flat mushrooms, peeled
4 teaspoons olive oil
4 slices rustic white bread
Small bunch of chives
6 eggs
3 tablespoons milk
Salt and cayenne pepper

1. Preheat the broiler.

2. Put 2 tablespoons of the butter into a nonstick saucepan ready for the scrambled eggs. Put the rest of the butter in a small bowl and beat with the chopped anchovies and a little pepper. Set aside.

3. Put the mushrooms, stalk side uppermost, on a piece of aluminum foil set on the broiler rack, with the edges of the foil turned up to catch the juices. Drizzle with the oil and sprinkle with a little salt and pepper. Broil under the broiler for 10 minutes, turning over halfway through cooking.

4. When the mushrooms are almost ready, toast the bread.

5. Chop some of the chives to produce about 3 tablespoons. Beat the eggs in a bowl with the milk, chopped chives, and a little salt and pepper.

6. Melt the butter in the saucepan, add the eggs, and cook over medium heat, stirring until scrambled.

7. Spread the toast with the anchovy butter and put onto serving plates. Top with the mushrooms, stalk side uppermost, and drizzle with any cooking juices. Spoon the scrambled egg on top and garnish with pieces of roughly chopped chives, if liked.

BALSAMIC-ROASTED TOMATOES

This simple brunch takes just 5 minutes to prepare and, as with all cooking, tastes only as good as the ingredients used. Choose tomatoes still on the vine for maximum flavor and the best balsamic vinegar that your budget will allow

SERVES 4

12 plum tomatoes, about 1 lb 6 oz
2 tablespoons olive oil
2 teaspoons balsamic vinegar
Small bunch of basil
2 tablespoons pine nuts
1 small ciabatta
Salt and ground black pepper

1. Preheat the oven to 350°F.

2. Halve the tomatoes and put cut side uppermost in a roasting pan. Drizzle with the oil and vinegar. Tear half the basil over the top, add the pine nuts, and season with salt and black pepper.

3. Roast in the preheated oven for 35–40 minutes, until tender.

4. Cut the ciabatta in half lengthwise then half again to give 4 quarters. Toast the cut side of the bread only, then transfer to serving plates and spoon the tomatoes on top. Sprinkle with the remaining basil leaves and serve immediately.

TIP
For garlic fans, rub the toast with a cut garlic clove before adding the tomatoes.

CROQUE MONSIEUR

A variation of this traditional French dish is the Croque
Madame, which is served topped with a fried egg.

SERVES 2

4 thick slices French bread
2 tablespoons butter, melted
¼ cup freshly grated Parmesan
   cheese
2 large slices of cured ham
1 cup shredded Emmental or similar
   Swiss cheese, about 4 oz

1. Using a pastry brush, brush one side of each slice of French bread
with the melted butter, then sprinkle with the Parmesan. Making sure
that the Parmesan-coated sides are on the outside, top two of the slices
with a slice of ham and half the Emmental each.

2. Top with the remaining two slices of French bread, Parmesan side
up, and toast in a sandwich grill for 4–5 minutes, or according to the
manufacturer's instructions, until the bread is golden and crispy and
the cheese is beginning to ooze from the sides. Serve immediately.

DEVILED MUSHROOMS

Buttery fried mushrooms are tossed in a spicy mix of Worcestershire sauce, whole-grain mustard, tomato paste, and, for those who like their food extra hot, a dash of Tabasco sauce.

SERVES 4

6 scallions
4 tablespoons butter
1 tablespoon sunflower oil
5⅔ cups sliced white mushrooms, about 14 oz
2 tablespoons Worcestershire sauce
2 teaspoons whole-grain mustard
2 teaspoons tomato paste
A few drops of Tabasco sauce (optional)
4 slices crusty bread
Salt and ground black pepper

1. Finely chop the scallions, reserving the green tops for garnish. Heat the butter and oil in a skillet, then add the white chopped scallion and the mushrooms. Fry for 3–4 minutes, stirring, until golden.

2. Stir in the Worcestershire sauce, mustard, and tomato paste. Add 4 tablespoons water, Tabasco, if using, and a little salt and black pepper. Cook for 2 minutes, stirring, until the sauce is beginning to thicken.

3. Toast the bread and put onto serving plates. Stir the green scallion tops through the mushrooms, cook for 1 minute, then spoon over the toast. Serve immediately.

DRINKS &
SWEET TREATS

COFFEE & CHOCOLATE STREUSEL CAKE

MAKES 16 SQUARES

⅓ cup self-rising flour
¼ cup superfine sugar
4 tablespoons butter, diced
⅓ cup roughly chopped hazelnuts
¼ cup slivered almonds
3½ oz dark chocolate, cut into chunks
Sifted confectioners' sugar,
   to decorate

CAKE

3 teaspoons instant coffee powder
2 teaspoons boiling water
12 tablespoons (1½ sticks) butter,
   at room temperature
¾ cup plus 2 tablespoons superfine
   sugar
3 eggs
1⅓ cups self-rising flour
1 teaspoon baking powder

1. Preheat the oven to 350°F. Cut a piece of nonstick parchment paper a little larger than a shallow 8-inch square baking pan. Snip diagonally into the corners of the paper, then press the paper into the pan to line the bottom and sides.

2. To make the streusel topping, put the flour, sugar, and butter into a bowl and blend in the butter until it resembles fine crumbs. Stir in the nuts and set the mixture aside.

3. To make the cake, mix the coffee and boiling water together in a cup until the coffee has dissolved. Cream the butter and sugar together in a large bowl until light. In a small bowl, lightly beat the eggs and, in a separate bowl, mix the flour and baking powder together.

4. Gradually beat the eggs and flour alternately into the butter mixture until it has all been added. Continue beating until smooth, then mix in the coffee.

5. Spoon the mixture into the lined pan and spread level. Sprinkle with the chocolate and then the streusel mixture. Bake in the preheated oven for 40–45 minutes, until the crumble is golden brown and a skewer inserted into the center of the cake comes out cleanly.

6. Let the cake cool slightly in the pan, then lift out using the lining paper. Peel away the paper, dust with a little sifted confectioners' sugar, and cut into squares. Serve warm or cold.

DATE & SODA BISCUITS

Made in the same way as Irish soda bread, these soft, crumbly biscuits are best eaten while still warm from the oven. Wrap in a napkin when they first come out to keep the crust soft. Plain yogurt can be used in place of the buttermilk.

MAKES 12

1½ cups whole-wheat flour
1 cup all-purpose or bread flour, plus extra for dusting
1½ teaspoons baking soda
Scant ⅓ cup light brown sugar
⅔ cup chopped dates
2 tablespoons butter, melted, plus extra for greasing
1 cup buttermilk
About 2 tablespoons milk
TO SERVE
Butter
Apricot jam

1. Preheat the oven to 425°F and lightly grease a baking sheet.

2. Put the flours, baking soda, and sugar into a mixing bowl. Add the dates and mix together.

3. Add the melted butter and buttermilk. Mix with a wooden spoon at first, then squeeze together with your hands to make a soft dough, adding the milk, if needed.

4. Knead lightly on a floured surface, then roll out to a thickness of 1 inch. Stamp out rounds with a plain 2½-inch cookie cutter. Place the rounds on the prepared baking sheet. Reroll the trimmings and continue rolling and shaping until all the dough has been used.

5. Dust the tops of the biscuits with a little extra flour, then bake in the preheated oven for 10–12 minutes, until the biscuies are browned and well risen.

6. Serve warm, split, and buttered with spoonfuls of apricot jam.

CARDAMOM COFFEE

SERVES 4

3 tablespoons strong, freshly ground
   coffee (South Indian, Colombian,
   or Javan)
1 teaspoon crushed cardamom seeds
1 cup milk
2 tablespoons sugar
2½ cups water

1. Place the coffee, cardamom, milk, sugar, and water in a large saucepan and bring to a boil. Simmer for 1–2 minutes, then, using a very fine-meshed strainer lined with cheesecloth, strain into a pitcher. Pour into glasses or mugs and serve hot.

LEMON GRASS TEA

SERVES 4

3–4 lemon grass stalks, finely
   chopped
4 teaspoons Indian tea leaves
   (Darjeeling or Assam)
3 cups water
TO SERVE:
Milk
Sugar

1. Put the lemon grass and tea leaves in a large saucepan with the water and bring to a boil. Lower the heat and simmer, uncovered, for 2–3 minutes. Strain and serve hot, adding milk and sugar to taste.

CHURROS WITH CHILI DIPPING SAUCE

Part of Spain's café culture, these tasty, doughnut-like cakes taste delicious with this Aztec-inspired dark chocolate sauce. Choose the medium-size mild red chiles found easily in the supermarket rather than the very fiery tiny Thai chiles or large Jamaican hot bonnet chiles.

SERVES 4

¼ teaspoon salt
⅓ cup superfine sugar
1¾ cups all-purpose flour
2 eggs
1 teaspoon vanilla extract
1 teaspoon ground cinnamon
Sunflower oil for deep-frying

CHILI DIPPING SAUCE

⅔ cup milk
½ mild red chile, seeded and roughly
  chopped
4 oz dark chocolate, broken into
  pieces
⅓ cup superfine sugar
1 tablespoon butter

1. Pour the milk for the sauce into a small saucepan and bring to a boil. Remove from the heat, add the chile, and let infuse for 30 minutes.

2. To make the churros, pour 1 cup water into a medium saucepan, add the salt and 1 tablespoon of the sugar, and bring just to a boil.

3. Take the pan off the heat, add the flour, and mix briefly. Return the pan to low heat and stir until the mixture comes together as a rough ball that leaves the sides of the pan almost clean. Let cool for 15 minutes.

4. Beat the eggs and vanilla together in a bowl. Mix the remaining sugar and cinnamon together in a second small bowl and set both aside.

5. To finish the sauce, strain the milk, discard the chile, then pour the milk back into the pan. Add the remaining sauce ingredients and heat together, stirring, until smooth and glossy but not boiling.

6. Gradually beat the egg mixture into the churros until smooth (use a food processor, if you have one). Spoon the mixture into a pastry bag fitted with a ½-inch wide plain tip.

TIP

If you want, make the churros dough the night before. Just place the dough in a plastic container, lay a piece of wetted parchment on the surface, replace the container lid, and chill in the refrigerator.

7. Pour the oil into a large saucepan to a depth of about 1 inch. Heat to 340°F on a kitchen thermometer. Alternately, pipe a tiny amount of the churros mixture into the oil; if the oil bubbles instantly, it is ready. Pipe spirals, "S" shapes, or squiggly lines into the oil in small batches, snipping the end of the churros with kitchen scissors. Cook for 2–3 minutes, until they float and are golden all over, turning over if needed.

8. Lift out of the pan with a slotted spoon and drain on paper towels. Continue piping and frying until all the mixture is used.

9. Transfer the churros to a plate lined with nonstick parchment paper and sprinkle with the cinnamon sugar.

10. Reheat the chili sauce if necessary, then pour into a shallow dipping bowl or individual bowls and serve with the warm churros.

BAKED NECTARINE WITH PISTACHIO YOGURT

Evocative of summery Mediterranean vacations, eat this alfresco, if you can, sitting in a sunny spot in the yard.

SERVES 4

4 nectarines, halved and pitted
2 tablespoons butter
2 tablespoons honey
⅓ cup pistachios, roughly chopped
1 scant cup whole-milk or Greek
   yogurt
Few drops of rose water
Rose petals, to decorate (optional)

1. Preheat the over to 350°F.

2. Put the nectarines, cut side uppermost in a small roasting pan. Cut the butter into eight and place a piece in the center of each peach. Drizzle with 1 tablespoon of the honey and sprinkle with one-third of the pistachios.

3. Bake the nectarines in the preheated oven for about 10 minutes, until hot and beginning to brown around the edges.

4. Meanwhile, put the yogurt into a bowl and stir in the remaining honey and pistachio nuts. Mix in a few drops of rose water to taste.

5. Spoon two nectarine halves per person onto serving plates, scooping up the juices from the bottom of the pan. Add spoonfuls of the pistachio yogurt and decorate with pale pink rose petals, if liked.

FRUIT SALAD KEBABS

Colorful pieces of pineapple, papaya, peach, and strawberry are marinated in a tangy sugar syrup flavored with star anise, an aromatic licorice-like spice often used in Chinese cookery. If you don't have any, ¼ teaspoon of ground five spice powder could be used instead—star anise is part of this spice mix.

SERVES 4

½ large pineapple
1 papaya
1 ripe peach, halved and pitted
8 large strawberries, hulled
Whole-milk or Greek yogurt,
    to serve

SYRUP

3 star anise or equivalent amount
    of broken pieces, crushed finely
    in a mortar and pestle
½ cup light brown sugar
Grated zest and juice of 1 lemon
½ cup water

1. Put all the syrup ingredients into a small saucepan. Bring slowly to a boil, stirring occasionally, until the sugar has dissolved, then boil rapidly for 1 minute. Set aside to cool slightly.

2. Cut the green top off the pineapple, then cut away the skin. Cut into eight wedges, cutting through the top down to the base. Remove the core, then thickly slice the wedges. Put the fruit into a shallow ceramic dish.

3. Quarter the papaya and scoop out the black seeds with a spoon. Peel away the skin, then thickly slice. Cut the peach into chunks and halve the strawberries. Mix all the fruit together in a bowl and pour the warm syrup over. Let infuse for 1 hour, or overnight, if preferred.

4. Preheat the broiler. Divide the fruit between eight metal skewers (or wooden skewers that have been soaked in cold water for 30 minutes) and cook under the preheated broiler for 8–10 minutes, turning several times and brushing with the syrup, until hot and browned around the edges.

5. Transfer to serving plates and serve with spoonfuls of yogurt mixed with a little of the syrup, if liked.

QUINOA & GOLDEN RAISIN PORRIDGE

Quinoa is one of those super foods—unusually for a grain, it contains all eight essential amino acids, it is gluten free, and is rich in calcium and iron, so it makes a very healthy start to the day.

SERVES 4

1½ cups quinoa flakes
2 cups milk
½ cup golden raisins
TO SERVE
2 bananas, sliced
1 orange, zest grated and flesh peeled
   and cut into segments
Ground cinnamon (optional)
Honey

1. Put the quinoa flakes into a saucepan with the milk, 1 cup water, and the golden raisins. Bring to a boil, stirring. Reduce the heat and simmer for 4–5 minutes, stirring frequently, until the quinoa is soft and the porridge thick and creamy.

2. Spoon the porridge into bowls immediately, because it will thicken with standing. Top with the bananas and orange segments, then sprinkle with the orange rind and a little ground cinnamon, if using. Finish with a drizzle of honey.

BANANA & CRANBERRY BREAD

If you have a couple of slightly overripe bananas in the fruit bowl, this is the perfect recipe to use them up. Just mash the bananas, add to the remaining ingredients, and fork together. What could be easier?

SERVES 4–6

Oil for greasing
1½ cups frozen cranberries
2–3 small ripe bananas, about 13 oz
   with the skins on
1 tablespoon lemon juice
2½ cups self-rising flour
1 teaspoon baking powder
¾ cup superfine sugar
¼ lb (1 stick) butter, melted
2 eggs, beaten

1. Preheat the oven to 325°F. Grease a 9 x 5 x 3-inch loaf pan with a little oil then line the bottom and two long sides with nonstick parchment paper. Put the cranberries into a microwave-proof bowl and cook on full power for 1½ minutes to defrost. Peel the bananas and mash them with the lemon juice.

2. Put the flour, baking powder, and sugar into a bowl. Add the bananas, the melted butter, and the eggs and fork together until smooth.

3. Stir in the cranberries, then spoon the mixture into the loaf pan. Spread the top level and bake in the preheated oven for 45–55 minutes, until the top is golden brown and has cracked slightly, and a skewer inserted into the center comes out cleanly.

4. Holding the pan with a dish towel, loosen the edge of the bread with a round-bladed knife. Turn out onto a cooling rack and let cool. Peel off the lining paper and serve thickly sliced.

OATMEAL & BERRIES

SERVES 2

1¼ cups rolled oats
⅔ cup milk
Handful of berries, such as
    raspberries, strawberries,
    blackberries, or cranberries,
    fresh, frozen and thawed,
    canned, or cooked

1. Place the oats in a saucepan with 2½ cups water and bring to a boil. Simmer for 10–20 minutes, stirring occasionally.

2. Add the milk, stir, and simmer for a few more minutes.

3. Serve with your chosen berries.

PUMPKIN SEED & APRICOT MUESLI

SERVES 2

½ cup rolled jumbo oats
1 tablespoon golden raisins or raisins
1 tablespoon pumpkin seeds
1 tablespoon chopped almonds
2 tablespoons chopped dried apricots
2 tablespoons fruit juice, such as
    apple or orange juice, or water
2 small apples, peeled and grated
3 tablespoons milk or plain yogurt

1. Place the oats, raisins, seeds, almonds, and apricots in a bowl with the fruit juice or water.

2. Add the grated apple and stir to mix. Top with milk or yogurt and serve.

OAT & APPLE FRUESLI

A perfect start to your morning, this wholesome brunch alternative will leave you feeling virtuous all day long!

SERVES 2

¼ cup rolled oats
¼ cup rolled wheat flakes
2 tablespoons sunflower seeds
2 tablespoons sweetened puffed quinoa
1 dried banana
2 dried apricots
5 slices crisp, dried apple, crumbled
¼ cup golden raisins
2 tablespoons dried, flaked coconut (optional)
2 tablespoons light brown sugar
¼ cup apple juice
¼ cup whole-milk yogurt, plus extra to serve
4 large slices cinnamon raisin bread
Glass of apple juice, to serve

1. Mix together all the dry ingredients in a bowl and stir in the apple juice and yogurt until well coated. Spoon onto two slices of cinnamon raisin bread and place the remaining two slices on top.

2. Put in a sandwich grill and toast for 2–3 minutes, or according to the manufacturer's instructions, until crisp and golden. Serve immediately with a bowl of yogurt and a glass of apple juice.

VANILLA STRACCIATELLE SMOOTHIE

A delicious vanilla-flavored yogurt smoothie, colored with specks of grated chocolate. It's a drinkable version of the Italian ice cream that has strands of chocolate running through it.

SERVES 2

2 cups vanilla-flavored yogurt
¾ cup cold milk
2 oz milk chocolate, coarsely grated

1. Put the yogurt into a food processor or blender with the milk and blend until frothy.

2. Pour the smoothie into a pitcher and stir in the grated chocolate. Serve immediately.

CARROT & HONEY BREAD

This yeast-free bread is easy to stir together and will keep in an airtight container for several days.

SERVES 6

Oil for greasing
¼ lb (1 stick) butter, plus extra
   to serve
½ cup honey
¼ cup light brown sugar
2 cups all-purpose flour
2 teaspoons baking powder
1 teaspoon ground cinnamon
1 generous cup muesli
2 carrots, about 7 oz, coarsely grated
¾ cup chopped dates
⅓ cup golden raisins
1 egg
½ cup milk
3 tablespoons sunflower seeds

1. Preheat the oven to 350°F. Grease a 9 x 5 x 3-inch loaf pan with a little oil and line the bottom and two long sides with a piece of nonstick parchment paper.

2. Put the butter, honey, and sugar into a saucepan and heat gently, stirring, until the butter has melted and the sugar dissolved, then take off the heat.

3. Put the flour, baking powder, cinnamon, and muesli into a bowl and mix together. Add the grated carrots, dates, and golden raisins and stir again.

4. Pour the honey mixture into the bowl. Add the egg and milk and stir together until well mixed.

5. Spoon the mixture into the prepared pan. Level the surface and sprinkle with the sunflower seeds.

6. Bake in the preheated oven for about 1 hour or until the top has cracked slightly and is golden brown, and a skewer comes out cleanly when inserted into the center of the bread.

7. Let cool in the pan for 10 minutes, then loosen the edges, turn out onto a cooling rack, and peel away the lining paper. Let cool completely, then serve sliced and spread with a little butter.

MARZIPAN TEA LOAF

Sometimes known as "bara brith" or "barm brack" this old-fashioned, fat-free fruit bread is made by soaking dried fruit in tea. Once made, it almost improves with keeping and can be served plain or spread with a little butter.

SERVES 4—6

Oil for greasing
2 cups mixed luxury dried fruits
1¼ cups warm tea
2⅓ cups self-rising flour
½ cup superfine sugar
2 apples, cored and grated
   (but not peeled)
1 egg
5 oz marzipan, diced

1. Put the dried fruit into a mixing bowl and pour over the warm tea. Let soak for 4 hours, or longer, if preferred.

2. Preheat the oven to 350°F. Grease a 9 x 5 x 3-inch loaf pan with a little oil, then line the bottom and two long sides with nonstick parchment paper.

3. Add the flour, sugar, grated apple, and egg to the soaked fruit and mix together well. Spoon about one-third into the loaf pan and sprinkle with half the diced marzipan. Repeat the layers, ending with the fruit mixture.

4. Smooth the top of the mixture and bake in the preheated oven for 1¼ hours, or until it is well risen, the top is golden and has cracked slightly, and a skewer comes out cleanly when inserted into the center of the cake.

5. Let cool in the pan for 10 minutes, then loosen the edges of the loaf and take out of the pan. Peel away the paper and allow to cool completely on a cooling rack. Serve thickly sliced.

OVEN-BAKED PECAN FRENCH TOAST

This is simplicity itself and takes just 10 minutes to prepare the night before. The fabulous aroma while it cooks is guaranteed to get even the most stubborn teenager out of bed.

SERVES 4–6

13 slices day-old bread
½ cup pecans, broken into pieces
1¾ cups milk
3 eggs
⅓ cup superfine sugar
1 teaspoon vanilla extract
1 teaspoon ground cinnamon
2 tablespoons butter, plus extra
    for greasing
Sifted confectioners' sugar, for
    dusting
TO SERVE
Maple syrup
Cream

1. Butter a 6-cup shallow, rectangular baking dish. Cut the day-old bread into 1-inch cubes, leaving the crust on. Place in the prepared baking dish and sprinkle with the pecans.

2. Lightly beat the milk, eggs, sugar, vanilla, and cinnamon together in a bowl, then strain over the bread so that it is coated in the milk mixture, pressing any remains through the strainer with the back of a spoon. Dot the top with the butter, cover with aluminum foil, and chill overnight in the refrigerator.

3. When ready to serve, preheat the oven to ~~350~~°F. Remove the aluminum foil from the dish and bake in the preheated oven for 30–35 minutes, until the top is golden and crispy and the custard is set. Check after 20–25 minutes and, if the bread seems to be browning too quickly, cover loosely with the foil for the remaining cooking time.

4. Dust with sifted confectioners' sugar and let stand for 10 minutes. Cut into large squares and transfer to serving plates. Serve warm drizzled with maple syrup and cream.

SWEET SOUTHERN ORANGE BISCUITS

These tangy biscuits are made not just with grated orange zest but with the juice, too. Serve with cream cheese and marmalade for adults, or a little butter and chocolate spread for children. The tops can also be sprinkled with a little ground cinnamon just before baking.

MAKES 12

3 cups self-rising flour
1 teaspoon baking powder
¼ cup superfine sugar, plus extra
    for sprinkling
4 tablespoons butter, diced, plus extra
    for greasing
Grated zest and juice of 1 orange
About ½ cup milk

TO SERVE

Cream cheese
Marmalade

1. Preheat the oven to 400°F. Grease a baking sheet with a little butter.

2. Put the flour, baking powder, sugar, and butter into a mixing bowl. Add the orange zest and blend the butter with your fingertips until the mixture resembles fine crumbs.

3. Add the orange juice, then gradually mix in enough milk to form a soft but not sticky dough. You may not need all the milk—it will depend on how juicy the orange is.

4. Knead lightly then roll out on a floured surface until the dough is about ¾ inch thick. Stamp out 2-inch circles with a cookie cutter, put the biscuits onto the prepared baking sheet, and reroll the trimmings. Continue cutting out biscuits and rerolling until all the dough is used.

5. Brush the top of the biscuits with a little milk and sprinkle with sugar. Bake in the preheated oven for 10–12 minutes, until well risen and golden brown. Transfer to a basket lined with a napkin and serve warm, split, and spread with cream cheese and marmalade.

PRUNES IN TEA WITH ORANGE YOGURT

You either love them or hate them, but either way prunes, which are also called dried plums, are incredibly good for you. Soak them in hot tea the night before, then just warm through the next morning before serving with a spoonful of yogurt mixed with orange zest and a drizzle of honey.

SERVES 4

2 cups pitted prunes
3 tablespoons superfine sugar
1 Earl Grey tea bag
1¾ cups boiling water
1 cup whole-milk yogurt
2 tablespoons honey
Grated zest of 1 orange

1. Put the prunes and sugar into a bowl, add the tea bag, and pour over the water. Mix together and let stand for 20 minutes, then remove the tea bag and transfer the bowl to the refrigerator overnight.

2. When ready to serve, transfer the prunes and soaking liquid to a saucepan and simmer over low heat for 5 minutes, until hot.

3. Meanwhile, mix the yogurt with the honey and two-thirds of the orange zest. Spoon the prunes into small bowls and top with spoonfuls of the yogurt sprinkled with a little of the remaining orange zest.

ALMOND & CRANBERRY BUNDT

German in origin, this rich buttery cake is luxuriously flavored with ground almonds, speckled with dried cranberries, and drizzled with glacé icing.

MAKES 12 SLICES

Oil for greasing
½ lb (2 sticks) butter, at room
   temperature
1 generous cup superfine sugar
4 eggs
1⅓ cups self-rising flour
1 scant cup ground almonds
½ teaspoon baking powder
½ teaspoon almond extract
2–3 tablespoons milk
Generous ½ cup dried cranberries

TO DECORATE
1 scant cup confectioners' sugar
3–4 teaspoons water
3 tablespoons slivered almonds,
   toasted

1. Preheat the oven to 350°F. Grease an 8-cup metal Bundt pan, then dust lightly with flour.

2. Cream the butter and sugar together in a bowl until light and fluffy. Beat in one egg then a little flour and continue beating in eggs and flour alternately until smooth. Stir in the remaining flour, ground almonds, baking powder, and almond extract, adding enough milk to produce a soft dropping consistency. Stir in the cranberries.

3. Spoon the mixture into the prepared pan or mold. Level the surface with a metal spatula and bake in the preheated oven for 50–60 minutes, until golden brown and a skewer comes out cleanly when inserted into the thickest part of the cake.

4. Let stand for 15 minutes, then loosen the edges, invert the pan or mold onto a cooling rack, and carefully remove. Let cool.

5. Sift the confectioners' sugar into a bowl, then gradually stir in enough water to make a thick, spoonable paste. Drizzle over the top of the cake, then sprinkle with the slivered almonds. Transfer to a plate or cutting board and let stand for about 15 minutes to let the icing harden.

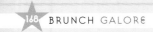

POMEGRANATE & ORANGE ENERGIZER

Sweet and fruity, with that unmistakable citrus zing, a glassful of this refreshing juice, packed with vitamin C, is just what you need to wake you up and get your system firing.

MAKES 1 GLASS

½ pomegranate
2 oranges, halved

1. Using a teaspoon, scoop the pomegranate seeds into a fine-mesh strainer placed over a bowl. Press the seeds with the back of the spoon to extract all the juice and then discard.

2. Squeeze the juice from the oranges and stir into the pomegranate juice. Pour into a glass and serve immediately

CHERRY-BERRY CLEANSER

Grapes are great cleansers, and the darker the skin, the more potent their cleansing properties. However, they are often sprayed heavily with pesticides, so it is best to buy organic ones if you can. The juice has an intense flavor, so you'll probably want to dilute it with a little water and serve poured over ice.

MAKES 1 SMALL GLASS

⅔ cup cherries, plus extra
   to decorate
¼ cup blueberries
½ cup black or red grapes
2–3 tablespoons water
Juice of ¼ lime

1. Remove the stalks and pits from the cherries. If you don't have a cherry pitter, cut around the crease of each cherry, gently pry the two halves apart and pull out the pits.

2. Push the cherries, blueberries, and grapes through a juicer and then dilute the juice with the water.

3. Add a squeeze of lime juice to taste and then pour the juice into a glass filled with ice cubes. Decorate with a cherry.

RED GRAPE & YOGURT BRÛLÉE

Lighter than a traditional crème brûlée, which is made with heavy cream, this version is not only lower in fat but it can be quicker to make, if you opt to mix store-bought vanilla pudding with creamy, thick yogurt.

SERVES 4

1¼ cups red seedless grapes, halved
⅔ cup custard or vanilla pudding
¾ cup Greek or whole-milk yogurt
½ teaspoon vanilla extract
3 tablespoons superfine sugar

1. Divide the red seedless grapes between four ⅔-cup individual ceramic ramekin dishes.

2. Mix the custard or pudding, yogurt, and vanilla extract together in a bowl. Spoon over the grapes and smooth the surface flat. Chill the mixture until required.

3. Sprinkle the sugar evenly over the tops of the dishes then caramelize with a kitchen torch. Alternatively, preheat the broiler. Stand the dishes in the bottom of the broiler pan, pack ice around, then brown under the preheated broiler. Serve within 20 minutes of making the topping.

MIXED BERRIES WITH SANGRIA

Rather than buying sangria, just mix a little red wine with some sugar and zingy citrus fruit zest for a light fresh twist on a fruity berry salad. To turn this into a dessert, spoon the citrus cream over a pavlova or individual meringue nests, then top with the berries.

SERVES 4

2½ cups, about 14 oz, hulled and
    thickly sliced strawberries
2 cups raspberries
6 tablespoons red wine
⅓ cup superfine sugar
Grated zest of 1 orange
Grated zest of 1 lemon
Mint leaves, to serve

CITRUS CREAM

1 cup heavy cream
Grated zest of ½ orange plus
    2 tablespoons juice
Grated zest of ½ lemon plus
    2 tablespoons juice
2 tablespoons superfine sugar

1. Put the berries into a serving bowl. Spoon over the wine, sugar, and fruit zests and mix together. Set aside for 30 minutes for the flavors to develop.

2. Just before serving, make the citrus cream by whipping the cream, fruit zest, and sugar together in a bowl until it forms soft swirls. Gradually beat in the fruit juice until thick once again. Spoon into a serving bowl.

3. Stir the mixed berries once again, then spoon into glasses, top with spoonfuls of the citrus cream, and decorate with mint.

HOT APPLE CAKE

SERVES 6–8

14 tablespooons (1¾ sticks) butter,
  at room temperature, plus extra
  for greasing
1 scant cup superfine sugar
Grated zest of 1 lemon and
  2 tablespoons of juice
3 eggs
2 cups self-rising flour
1 teaspoon baking powder
3 large apples, about 1 lb
Good quality toffee sauce or dolche
  de leche, to serve

TOPPING

1 tablespoon butter, melted
1 tablespoon superfine sugar

TIP

*To make toffee sauce, heat
4 tablespoons each of butter, corn
syrup, and sugar over a low heat, stirring
until melted. Increase the heat slightly and
cook for 1–2 minutes, until the mixture begins
to darken slightly in color. Remove from the
heat, gradually stir in 1 cup heavy cream,
then return to the stove. Cook for
2–3 minutes, stirring all the time.
Mix in 2 tablespoons lemon juice
and let cool.*

1. Preheat the oven to 350°F. Butter a 9-inch springform cake pan and line the bottom with a circle of nonstick parchment paper.

2. To make the cake, beat the butter and sugar together in a large bowl until light and creamy, then add the lemon zest.

3. Beat the eggs in a small bowl. Mix the flour and baking powder together in a separate bowl. Beat alternate spoonfuls of egg, then flour into the creamed mixture, beating well after each addition until the mixture is smooth.

4. Peel, core, and slice the apples. Toss with the lemon juice, then stir two-thirds into the cake mixture. Spoon into the prepared pan.

5. Spread the top of the cake level then sprinkle with the remaining apple slices. Brush with the melted butter and sprinkle with 1 tablespoon sugar, then cook in the preheated oven for 55–65 minutes, until golden brown and a skewer inserted into the center of the cakes comes out cleanly. You may need to cover the top of the cake with a piece of aluminum foil toward the end of cooking if it seems to be overbrowning.

6. Let the cake cool for 10 minutes in the pan, then loosen the edge and remove the pan. Peel away the parchment paper and put onto a cooling rack. Serve warm or cold, cut into wedges, with a drizzle of toffee sauce.

TROPICAL FRUIT SALAD

Packed with vitamin C, this colorful fruit salad not only looks good but does you good. For extra goodness serve with yogurt and honey.

SERVES 4

1 mango
1 papaya
4 kiwifruit
1 fresh coconut
Grated zest of 1 lime
Juice of 2 limes
3 tablespoons superfine sugar

1. Preheat the broiler to a moderate heat and line the broiler rack with aluminum foil.

2. Cut a thick slice off each side of the mango to reveal the large, flat, oval pit. Cut the flesh away from the pit, peel, and cut into long slices.

3. Cut the papaya in half lengthwise and scoop out the small black seeds. Peel and cut into long slices. Peel the kiwifruit and cut into wedges.

4. Put all the fruits into a serving bowl. Pierce one of the three eyes at the top of the coconut with a small sharp knife—only one will pierce easily so try each in turn until you can make a small hole. Enlarge the hole, then shake the coconut juice over the fruits.

5. Add the lime zest, half the lime juice, and 2 tablespoons of the sugar to the fruits and toss gently together.

6. Crack open the coconut shell. Using a small knife, lever away the outer shell from half the coconut. Pare the coconut flesh into thin ribbons with a vegetable peeler. Put onto the foil-lined broiler rack in a single layer and sprinkle lightly with the remaining sugar and lime juice.

7. Cook under the preheated broiler for 2–3 minutes, until just turning golden brown. Sprinkle over the salad and serve.

CHOC-ORANGE TORTE

SERVES 6—8

Oil for greasing
2 sweet potatoes, about 14 oz,
    cut into large dice
Grated zest and juice of 1 orange
1⅔ cups self-rising flour
½ cup unsweetened cocoa
1 teaspoon baking soda
12 tablespoons (1½ sticks) butter,
    at room temperature
¾ cup light brown sugar
3 eggs
Orange segments, to serve
FROSTING
7 oz dark chocolate, broken into
    chunks
¾ cup heavy cream
Grated zest of 1 orange

1. Preheat the oven to 325°F. Grease a 9-inch springform cake pan with a little oil and line the bottom with nonstick parchment paper.

2. Steam the sweet potato over a saucepan of boiling water for 15 minutes, until tender. Mash until smooth, then mix with the orange zest and juice and let cool for 15 minutes.

3. Sift the flour, cocoa, and baking soda into a bowl. Cream the butter and sugar together in a large mixing bowl until light and fluffy. Gradually beat in the eggs alternately with the flour, until all have been added and the mixture is smooth. Stir in the mashed sweet potato and mix well.

4. Spoon into the prepared pan. Spread the top level and bake in the preheated oven for 45—55 minutes, until well risen, the top is slightly cracked, and a skewer comes out cleanly when inserted into the center.

5. Let cool in the pan for 15 minutes, then loosen the edge and remove the pan and lining paper. Put on a cooling rack and cool completely.

6. To make the frosting, put the chocolate and cream in a bowl set over a saucepan of gently simmering water and heat for about 5 minutes, beating lightly from time to time, until the chocolate has melted and the frosting is thick and glossy. Remove from the heat. Cool for 5—10 minutes, beating occasionally, until thick enough to hold its shape.

7. Spoon the frosting over the cake and spread with a knife. Decorate with grated orange zest, then put in a cool place for about an hour for the frosting to harden. Cut into slices and serve with the orange segments.

MELON WITH GINGERED GREEN TEA

A refreshingly light fruit salad that is best made in summer, when the melons have the most flavor. This can be made either just before you are ready to serve or the night before, if that suits you better, and chilled in the refrigerator.

SERVES 4

2 teaspoons loose green tea
1 cup boiling water
2 tablespoons honey
4 teaspoons preserved ginger syrup
1 piece preserved ginger
1 galia melon
1 charentais melon

1. Put the tea into a teapot, pour over the boiling water, and let infuse for 3–4 minutes.

2. Strain the tea into a serving bowl, stir in the honey and ginger syrup, and let cool.

3. Finely chop the piece of preserved ginger. Cut the melons in half and scoop out the seeds with a spoon. Cut the melons into thick slices, remove the peel, and cut the flesh into chunks.

4. Add the melon to the tea, toss together gently, and sprinkle with the chopped ginger. Chill, and serve spooned into glasses.

APRICOT PARFAIT WITH GRANOLA

SERVES 4

GRANOLA

Vegetable oil for greasing
2 tablespoons sunflower oil
2 tablespoons butter
2 tablespoons honey
2 tablespoons light brown sugar
2 tablespoons sesame seeds
2 tablespoons sunflower seeds
2 tablespoons pumpkin seeds
¼ cup rolled oats

APRICOT PARFAIT

1 generous cup dried apricots
1½ cups low-fat plain yogurt
2 tablespoons light brown sugar

1. Preheat the oven to 350°F and grease a baking sheet with a little vegetable oil.

2. To make the granola, heat the sunflower oil, butter, honey, and sugar in a small saucepan until just melted. Stir in the remaining ingredients and mix well.

3. Turn the mixture out onto the prepared baking sheet. Press into a thin, even layer and bake in the preheated oven for 6–8 minutes, until golden brown all over. Check halfway through cooking and turn the baking sheet, if necessary, so that the granola cooks evenly.

4. Let the granola cool for 5 minutes, then loosen with a spatula and let cool completely.

5. Meanwhile, put the apricots into a small saucepan with 1 cup water. Cover and simmer for 10 minutes, until the apricots are tender and plumped up. Puree in a blender until smooth, adding a little extra water if necessary. Let cool.

6. Stir the yogurt and sugar together in a bowl. Spoon into four small tumblers and gently swirl through spoonfuls of apricot puree. Sprinkle a little broken granola on top and serve the remaining granola broken into large shards propped up against the glasses.

SAFFRON CUSTARD WITH BROILED PLUMS

SERVES 4

2 eggs plus 2 egg yolks
3 tablespoons superfine sugar
2½ cups milk
⅛ teaspoon saffron strands
8 red plums, about 14 oz, pitted
   and thickly sliced
Juice of 1 orange
2 tablespoons butter
¼ cup light brown sugar
2 pieces preserved ginger, cut into
   thin strips

TIP
*If you don't have any
individual metal pudding
molds, then cook the custards
in small ceramic ovenproof
ramekins or individual
soufflé dishes.*

1. Preheat the oven to 350°F. Put four ¾-cup individual metal pudding molds into a roasting pan and line the bottom of each with a small circle of nonstick parchment paper.

2. Put the eggs, egg yolks, and sugar into a bowl and mix together with a fork. Pour the milk into a saucepan, bring just to a boil, then gradually beat into the egg mixture.

3. Strain the milk mixture back into the saucepan. Add the saffron strands and stir well. Let stand for 15 minutes.

4. Stir the cooled custard once more then pour into the molds. Pour warm water into the roasting pan to come halfway up the sides of the molds.

5. Place, uncovered, in the preheated oven for 25–30 minutes, until the custards are set. Lift the molds out of the roasting pan with a cloth. Let cool, then transfer to the refrigerator overnight.

6. When almost ready to serve, preheat the broiler and line the broiler pan with aluminum foil, folding up the edges to make a dish. Add the plums, drizzle with the orange juice, dot with the butter, and sprinkle with the sugar and ginger. Broil for 5 minutes, until the plums are hot and just beginning to brown around the edges.

7. Run a knife around the edges of the custards, then turn out. Peel off the lining paper. Arrange on serving plates, spoon the hot plums around the custards, and drizzle over a little of the plum juices.

MANGO & MINT SHERBET

SERVES 4

3 ripe mangoes, peeled, pitted, and
   coarsely chopped
¼ cup lemon juice
1 tablespoon sugar
12 mint leaves, finely chopped
3 cups ice water
Ice cubes

1. Put the mango, lemon juice, sugar, and mint leaves in a food processor or blender with the water and blend until smooth. To serve, pour into ice-filled glasses.

SPICY TOMATO JUICE

SERVES 1–2

2 medium tomatoes, about 10 oz
3 medium celery sticks, about 4 oz
1-inch piece of fresh ginger root,
   roughly chopped
1 garlic clove
1-inch piece of fresh horseradish,
   roughly chopped
2 medium carrots, about 6 oz
2 ice cubes
Celery slivers, to decorate (optional)

1. Place all the ingredients in a food processor or blender and blend until smooth. Blend with 2 ice cubes and serve in a glass. Decorate with celery slivers, if liked.

BAKED HONEYED PEACHES

This is a delightful summer dish that is really quick and easy to make. It also works equally as well with nectarines or plums.

SERVES 4

4 tablespoons butter, plus extra
   for greasing
4 large ripe peaches, halved and
   pitted
½ cup slivered almonds
¼ cup honey
Ground cinnamon, for dusting
Sour cream, to serve

1. Preheat the oven to 400°F. Butter a shallow baking dish large enough to take the peaches.

2. Place the peaches in the baking dish, skin side down. Dot with the butter, then sprinkle with the almonds, drizzle with the honey, and dust with a little cinnamon.

3. Bake at the top of the preheated oven for 10–15 minutes, until the peaches are turning color and the almonds have lightly browned.

4. Serve the peaches with the juices drizzled over, and topped with a spoonful of sour cream.

CONVERSION CHARTS

To help you enjoy these recipes wherever you live, here is a list of key easy-to-follow conversions that have been rounded up or down. To ensure the best results, never mix your measures—choose either imperial and cups or metric—and stay with that system. Cup measures are based on the American imperial measuring cup. One American cup holds 8 fl oz, 16 tablespoons, or 240 ml.

OVEN TEMPERATURE

°Farhenheit	°Celcius	Gas mark
225°F	110°C	¼
250°F	120°C	½
275°F	135°C	1
300°F	150°C	2
325°F	160°C	3
350°F	180°C	4
375°F	190°C	5
400°F	200°C	6
425°F	220°C	7
450°F	230°C	7

* Used for frying:
325°F (160°C) / 340°F (170°C)

LIQUID CONVERSIONS

American	Imperial	Metric
1 teaspoon	1 teaspoon	5 ml
1 tablepoon	½ fl oz	15 ml
2 tablepoons	1 fl oz	30 ml
¼ cup	2 fl oz	60 ml
⅓ cup	2¾ fl oz	85 ml
½ cup	4 fl oz	120 ml
¾ cup	6 fl oz	180 ml
1 cup	8 fl oz	240 ml
1¼ cups	½ pint	300 ml
2½ cups	1 pint	600 ml
3 cups	1¼ pints	750 ml
4 cups	1¾ pints	1 liter

WEIGHTS

Imperial	Metric
¼ oz	10 g
½ oz	15 g
¾ oz	20 g
1 oz	25 g
4 oz	115 g
4½ oz	125 g
6 oz	175 g
7 oz	200 g
8 oz	225 g
12 oz	340 g
1 lb	450 g
1½ lb	675 g
2¼ lb	1 kg

BUTTER CONVERSIONS

Imperial	Metric
1 tablespoon	15 g
2 tablespoons (¼ stick)	25 g
3 tablespoons	40 g
4 tablespoons (½ stick)	60 g
5 tablespoons	75 g
6 tablespoons (¾ stick)	85 g
7 tablespoons	100 g
8 tablespoons (¼ pound, 1 stick)	115 g
9 tablespoons	125 g
10 tablespoons	140 g
12 tablespoons	170 g
14 tablespoons (1¾ sticks)	200 g
1 cup (½ pound, 2 sticks)	225 g
18 tablespoons	250 g
2 cups (1 pound, 4 sticks)	450 g

DIMENSIONS

Imperial	Metric
1 inch	2.5 cm
2 inches	5 cm
3¼ inches	8 cm
3½ inches	9 cm
4 inches	10 cm
5 inches	12.5 cm
7 inches	18 cm
8 inches	20 cm
9 inches	23 cm
10 inches	25.5 cm
11 inches	27.5 cm
12 inches	30 cm
13½ inches	34 cm

US CUP CONVERSIONS

1 US cup	Metric
almonds, ground	95 g
almonds, slivered	110 g
arugula	20 g
berries, mixed and strawberry	150 g
berries, raspberries and blueberries	145 g
cheese, soft, such as cream cheese, mascarpone	220 g
cheese, semihard, grated	115 g
cocoa, unsweetened	110 g
corn, kernels	210 g
cornmeal	170 g
black-eye peas	200 g
dried fruits, such as currants, raisins, sultanas	145 g
dried fruits, chopped, such as dates, apricots	175 g
flour, all-purpose/self-rising	150 g
flour, rice	160 g
flour, wholewheat	125 g
grapes	160 g
jelly, jam, marmalade	320 g
peas, frozen	150 g
nuts, whole	145 g
nuts, mixed and chopped	115 g
rice, short-grain uncooked	200 g
rice, long-grain uncooked	185 g
rolled oats	100 g
salad leaves	50 g
sugar, caster/granulated	200 g
sugar, packed brown	220 g
sugar, confectioners'	140 g
fresh berries	150 g

GLOSSARY

US term	British term
all-purpose flour	plain flour
arugula	rocket
bacon, Canadian-style	bacon, back
bell pepper	pepper or capsicum
beets	beetroot
broiler	grill
caster sugar	superfine sugar
cherries, candied	cherries, glacé
chocolate, dark	chocolate, plain
cilantro	coriander
confectioners' sugar	icing sugar
corn syrup	golden syrup
cornmeal	polenta
cornstarch	cornflour
coconut, shredded	desiccated coconut
crackers, graham	biscuits, digestive
cream, heavy	cream, double
drop biscuit	drop scone
fave beans	broad beans
flour, all-purpose	flour, plain
flour, self-rising	flour, self-raising
gherkin pickles	cornichons

US term	British term
ginger, stem	ginger, preserved
sponge toffee	honeycomb
jam	conserve
jelly	jam
mushrooms, white	mushrooms, button
onion, Bermuda	onion, sweet white
paper, parchment	paper, baking
pitted	stoned
raisins, golden	sultanas
scallions	spring onions
scones	biscuits
self-rising flour	self-raising flour
shrimp	prawns
skillet	frying pan
sugar, confectioners'	sugar, icing
sugar, superfine	sugar, caster
sugar, turbinado	sugar, demerara or raw
vanilla pudding	custard
wrap, platic	clingfilm
yogurt, plain	yogurt, natural
zest	peel
zucchini	courgette

INDEX